Peter Harrison's
PC CRASH COURSE SERIES

British authors!

CW01081677

Microsoft Word 97
Advanced Course

Your Personal
PC
TRAINING
COURSEWARE

Microsoft Word 97
Advanced Course

ISBN: 1873005342 ~ 01/12/98

Welcome!

Thank you for choosing this book. A team of authors and editors at **PC Productions** has worked together to develop the course to the highest standards. We continually monitor the style of writing and check that instructions and exercises work properly. Our aim is to provide course material that is easy to understand and use - it should also be an effective learning tool for the user. We hope that you will be fully satisfied with this course.

PC Productions publishes a large range of computer books and training courseware with over 150 titles in all. More information is available through your local book shop or dealer.

PC Productions Limited
Dudbridge Road
Stroud
GL5 3HT
England

Published by
PC Productions Limited

Printed and bound
in England

Quick Reference

Study instructions

Items with a round bullet are instructions that you should follow. For example:

● Open the **File** menu and choose **Close.**

Other indented, bulleted items are information only - they should not be treated as instructions. For example:

    ✥ To close a document, open the **File** menu and choose **Close**

Running text may contain explanations or supplementary information.

Using the mouse

Most application programs these days make extensive use of the mouse. There are a few mouse operations that you should be familiar with:

Operation	Description
Point	To point using the mouse, simply move your mouse across your desk or mouse mat. The mouse pointer on the screen will follow the movement. If you run out of space, just lift the mouse, move it and put it down again, then carry on moving it.
Click	To click an object means that you should point at the desired object and press the LEFT-HAND mouse button ONCE.
Right-click	As for Click above, but using the RIGHT-HAND mouse button instead.
Double-click	As for Click above, but press the LEFT-HAND mouse button TWICE in quick succession. If you do this too slowly, your computer will interpret this as two single clicks.
Drag	First position the mouse pointer over an object, then press the left-hand mouse button down and hold it down while you move the mouse around. The object will be dragged around until you release the mouse button.

Table of Contents

Chapter 1 ~ Introduction

Welcome to the *Microsoft Word 97 Advanced Course*. This course follows on from the *Microsoft Word 97 Intermediate Course*. Although it is not necessary for you to have followed the Intermediate Course, it is assumed that you are able to perform certain tasks. These are listed in the next section - *What you need to know*.

It is not intended that this course should simply replace the original documentation supplied with your software. It is designed to guide you through the most important features of the program, using language that is easy to understand and examples that are easy to follow.

You can read about the following in this chapter:

    ♭   What you need to know

    ♭   The course objectives

What you need to know

As this is an advanced course, it is assumed that you have a working knowledge of Word and can perform certain basic tasks. You should know how to:

    ♭   Start and exit Word.

    ♭   Use the menus, toolbar buttons and shortcut key combinations; change and zoom the view; show and hide toolbars.

    ♭   Create new documents using both the **New** button and the **File**, **New** menu option; type text and correct mistakes using the Spelling and Grammar checker; use the Thesaurus.

    ♭   Open, save, print and close documents; use Print Preview to view a document as it would be printed.

- ✍ Select words, phrases and paragraphs; change the appearance of text; use the Format Painter to copy formats from one item of text to another; use the Highlight feature to highlight text; modify paragraphs and use the bullets, numbering and line spacing features.

- ✍ Use paragraph styles, templates and Wizards.

- ✍ Undo and redo any changes you make to a document.

- ✍ Edit your documents; insert the date and time, and special symbols such as ☑ and ⊠; add headers and footers to a document.

- ✍ Use the automation features AutoCorrect, AutoText, AutoFormat, AutoComplete and AutoSummarize to speed up the production of your documents.

- ✍ Copy and move text within a single document and between different documents.

- ✍ Search for words or phrases throughout your documents and replace them with other words or phrases as appropriate; use the Go To feature and the Select Browse Object menu to navigate your document.

- ✍ Set up tabs and produce basic tables.

- ✍ Set up and use Mail Merge to create standard letters, and link them to data files for mass mailing.

Course objectives

By the end of this course you will be able to:

- ✍ Add borders and shading to text using both the Tables and Borders toolbar and the Borders and Shading dialog box.

- ✍ Create a table; add text before it; insert and delete rows; merge and delete cells; use formulae within a table; AutoFormat a table; convert a table to text.

- Sort the contents of a table; sort the paragraphs of a document.

- Change the number and width of columns in a document; add vertical lines between columns; have a different number of columns in the same document.

- Insert a picture; scale the picture and move and resize it; wrap text around the picture; add a text box, including adding a text box to existing text; wrap text around the text box.

- Bring all these desktop publishing skills together to create articles.

- Use heading styles; number headings; use the Outline view to view and rearrange a document; insert a table of contents.

- Manage files on your exercise diskette and hard drive; enter and view document properties and statistics; create new folders and shortcuts; use Favorites; insert a file in a document; rename and delete documents; send documents to the A drive; work with groups of files.

- Search for files using a range of simple and more advanced criteria; save, open and edit a search.

- Save documents with up to three levels of security - Read-only recommended, Password to modify and Password to open; set your system to do automatic saves and back ups.

- Create a letter template both on your exercise diskette and on your hard drive; open a template in the New dialog box and use it to complete a document; delete a template.

- Write simple macros to automate tasks you perform frequently in Word.

Notes

Use this page to make notes of your own.

Page #   Notes

_____ _____

_____ _____

_____ _____

_____ _____

_____ _____

_____ _____

_____ _____

_____ _____

_____ _____

_____ _____

_____ _____

_____ _____

_____ _____

_____ _____

_____ _____

Chapter 2 ~ Borders & Shading

Word provides an attractive feature that allows you to put a border around a paragraph. You can also add some background shading.

In this chapter you will learn about:

ᴥ   Using the **Borders** button in the Formatting toolbar

ᴥ   Using the Tables and Borders toolbar

ᴥ   Adding borders to paragraphs

ᴥ   Background shading

ᴥ   Using the Borders and Shading dialog box

ᴥ   Adding a page border

To get started

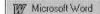 ●   Start your Word program.

 ●   If the Office Assistant is displayed at any time throughout this chapter, you should read what it has to say and then close it — click the **Close** button in the Office Assistant window.

 ●   Open the **Heart of a Computer** document from your exercise diskette.

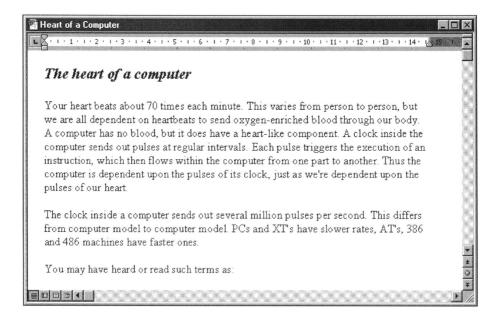

The heart of a computer

Your heart beats about 70 times each minute. This varies from person to person, but we are all dependent on heartbeats to send oxygen-enriched blood through our body. A computer has no blood, but it does have a heart-like component. A clock inside the computer sends out pulses at regular intervals. Each pulse triggers the execution of an instruction, which then flows within the computer from one part to another. Thus the computer is dependent upon the pulses of its clock, just as we're dependent upon the pulses of our heart.

The clock inside a computer sends out several million pulses per second. This differs from computer model to computer model. PCs and XT's have slower rates, AT's, 386 and 486 machines have faster ones.

You may have heard or read such terms as:

Adding borders

There are three ways of adding borders to a paragraph:

↳ Click the downward-pointing arrow of the **Borders** button in the Formatting toolbar, then click the button which represents the border position you require, e.g., **Top**, **Bottom**, **Left**, **Right**, **Inside** or **Outside**

↳ Click the **Tables and Borders** button in the Standard toolbar to display the Tables and Borders toolbar, where you can choose a border style, position and colour

↳ Open the **Format** menu and choose **Borders and Shading** to display the Borders and Shading dialog box, where several attributes can be set

You will try the first method now.

Using the Borders button

A paragraph can be attractively emphasised by putting a box around it. Just move the insertion point to the desired paragraph and then use the **Borders** button to add a border to it. If you want to add a border around more than one paragraph, just select the desired paragraphs first.

- Position the insertion point anywhere in the second paragraph starting The clock inside.

Click here

- Click the downward-pointing arrow of the **Borders** button in the Formatting toolbar.

A box of further border buttons is displayed.

- Point the mouse at each of the border buttons, without clicking them, and read what each one represents.

- In the box of border buttons, click the **Outside Border** button.

A box is added around the paragraph.

Click here

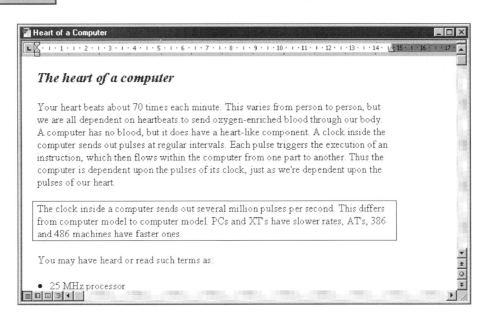

Removing a border using the Borders button

There are various ways of removing a border. Two simple methods are:

     ✎   Click the depressed **Borders** button in the Formatting toolbar

     ✎   Click the downward-pointing arrow in the **Borders** button to open the box of border buttons, then click the **No Border** button

●   Click the depressed **Borders** button in the Formatting toolbar to toggle the border off.

The border is removed from the paragraph.

The Tables and Borders toolbar

Another way of adding borders is to use the Tables and Borders toolbar. This has buttons and list boxes which enable you to add borders and to change the line style around the borders. You can also add shading effects to your paragraphs.

To display the Tables and Borders toolbar, you just need to click the **Tables and Borders** button in the Standard toolbar. If the Tables and Borders toolbar is already displayed on your screen you can ignore the next instruction (you can check the picture below to see what it looks like).

●   If the Tables and Borders toolbar is not displayed, click the **Tables and Borders** button to display it now.

The Tables and Borders toolbar should now be displayed. You may also find that your mouse pointer has changed to a small pen - Word thinks that you wish to draw a table.

●   If the mouse pointer has changed to a pen, press **Esc** to see the normal mouse pointer.

You may also at this stage have to close the Office Assistant.

- If necessary, click the **Close** button in the Office Assistant window.

The Tables and Borders toolbar may appear as a *docked* or a *floating* toolbar. The picture below shows the toolbar as a *floating* toolbar. It doesn't matter how the Tables and Border toolbar is displayed, as long as you can see all of the buttons and list boxes.

- Point the mouse at each of the toolbar buttons, without clicking them, to see what each one does.

Adding another paragraph border

You can now add a paragraph border using the Tables and Borders toolbar. However, before doing so, it is important to note that the line style used for the border is the line style shown in the **Line Style** list box, and that the weight for the line is that shown in the **Line Weight** list box. First, you will set the required line style and line weight for your border.

> *You cannot change the line style and weight of a border once it has been applied. You have to first remove the border and then choose the required style and weight before reapplying the border.*

- Open the **Line Style** list box.

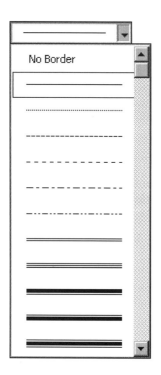

- Choose the first double line in the drop-down list.

- Open the **Line Weight** list box.

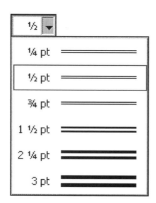

- Choose the **1 ½ pt** line weight.

You can now add the border to your paragraph.

- Make sure that your insertion point is still in the second paragraph.

- In the Tables and Borders toolbar, click the **Outside Border** button – click the main button itself and *not* the downward-pointing arrow.

The paragraph now has a double line border.

- Click the downward-pointing arrow of the **Borders** button.

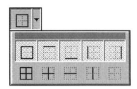

Notice how the **Outside Border**, **Top Border**, **Bottom Border**, **Left Border** and **Right Border** buttons are all depressed: adding an outside border is the same as adding borders to the top, bottom, left and right. Using the **Left Border** and **Right Border** buttons, you can now remove just the left and right lines.

- With the insertion point still in the second paragraph, click the **Left Border** button.

- Click the downward pointing arrow of the **Borders** button once more, and then click the **Right Border** button.

The paragraph now has a double line above and below it.

The clock inside a computer sends out several million pulses per second. This differs from computer model to computer model. PCs and XT's have slower rates, AT's, 386 and 486 machines have faster ones.

Shading a paragraph

As well as adding a border, you can use the Tables and Borders toolbar to apply shading or a colour to a paragraph. You can apply shading with or without a border. Format the title and add shading as follows:

- Select the whole title <u>The heart of a computer</u>.

- Open the **Font Size** list box and choose **24**.

- Click the **Center** button or press **Ctrl+E**.

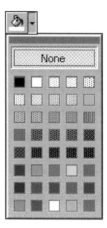

- In the Tables and Borders toolbar, click the downward-pointing arrow of **Shading Color** button.

A list of shades and colours that can be applied to the paragraph is displayed.

- Choose **Gray - 30%**.

- Click anywhere on the document to remove the selection highlight.

You have now applied shading to the title.

The heart of a computer

Unlike with the line style, you can change the shading or colour by just choosing another one.

- Click anywhere on the title.

- Click the downward-pointing arrow of the **Shading Color** button and choose **Yellow**.

The background shading for the heading is now coloured yellow. Next, you will remove the shading altogether.

- Click the downward-pointing arrow of the **Shading Color** button and choose **None**.

Finally, you will hide the Tables and Borders toolbar.

- Click the **Tables and Borders** button in the Standard toolbar.

The Tables and Borders toolbar is hidden.

Using the Borders and Shading dialog box

All of the features on the Tables and Borders toolbar, and a few more, are available in the Borders and Shading dialog box.

●   `Click anywhere on the title.`

●   `Open the` **`Format`** `menu and choose` **`Borders and Shading`**`.`

The Borders and Shading dialog box is displayed. There are three sets of options: **Borders**, **Page Border** and **Shading**.

●   `If necessary, click the` **`Borders`** `tab to show those options.`

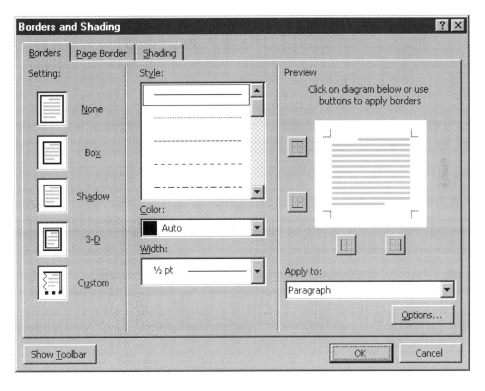

There are five pre-set formats allowing you to choose no border, a simple box border, a box border with a shadow behind it, a 3-D border and a Custom border. You can also choose a line style, colour and width for the border.

●   `In the` <u>`Setting`</u> `options, choose` **`Shadow`**`.`

Your choice can be seen in the <u>Preview</u> box. You will now make the border line thicker and then change the colour.

● Open the <u>Width</u> list box and choose **3pt**.

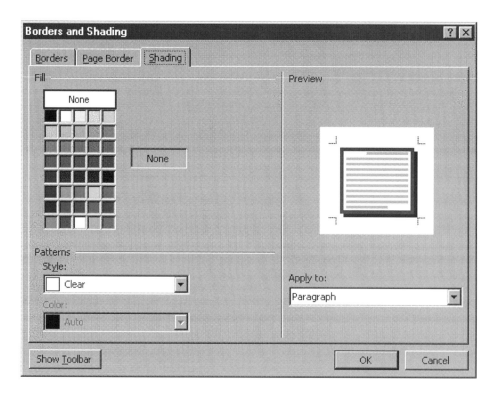

● Open the <u>Color</u> list box and choose **Blue**.

All the lines are now blue.

● Click **OK**.

The heading now has a thick blue box with a black shadow. Next, you will change a few shading options.

● Open the **Format** menu and choose **Borders and Shading**.

● Click the **Shading** tab to show those options.

As well as the different shading options that were available in the Tables and Borders toolbar, you can also set a pattern style and colour.

● In the <u>Fill</u> list, choose **Gray - 25%**.

● In the <u>Patterns</u> options, open the <u>Color</u> list box and choose **Yellow**.

- Click **OK**.

The heading now has a light yellow shading.

You can combine the Fill and Patterns colour options to create different colours and effects.

Try this:

- Open the **Format** menu and choose **Borders and Shading**.

The Shading options should be displayed.

- In the Fill list, choose **Red**.

The Preview box shows a bright orange colour now. The yellow and red have combined with the yellow, or foreground colour, set to 25%.

- Open the Style list box and choose **80%**.

The yellow colour is now set to 80%, making the overall colour a lot closer to yellow than to orange. If you choose one of the other style options, e.g., Lt Grid, the lines are in the colour indicated in the Patterns Color list box.

- Open the Style list box and choose **Lt Grid**.

- Click **OK**.

The chosen shading is applied to the paragraph. You might want to change it again on your own!

Adding a page border

Finally, you will add a border to the pages in your document. The options in the Borders and Shading dialog box should be familiar to you by now, so only brief instructions are given.

- Open the **Format** menu and choose **Borders and Shading**.

- Click the **Page Border** tab to show those options.

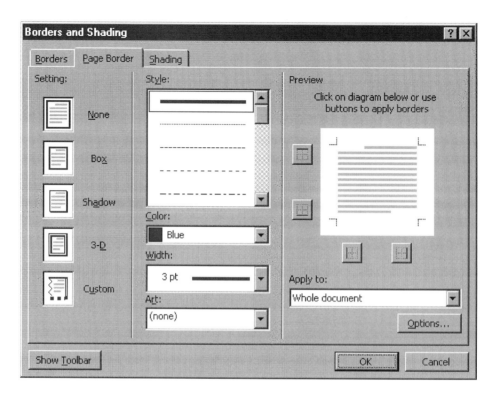

- In the Setting options, choose **Box**.

- Open the Color list box and choose **Red**.

- Click **OK**.

You can now use Print Preview to view the borders.

- Open the **File** menu and choose **Print Preview**, or click the **Print Preview** button.

The two pages in the document have a red border.

- When you are ready, close the Print Preview view - click the **Close** button in the Print Preview toolbar.

Ending the session

You have now completed the tutorial in this chapter. There is an additional exercise that you may wish to do before moving on to the next chapter or exiting Word. First, you should close the current document.

- Open the **File** menu and choose **Close** - choose **No** to avoid saving the changes.

- If you are not continuing directly with the extra exercise or the next chapter and want to stop now, open the **File** menu and choose **Exit** to exit Word.

Exercise 2a

- Open the **Appointment of Clerical Assistant** document from your exercise diskette.

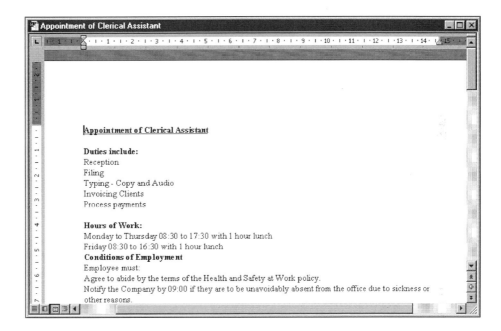

First, change the format of the heading and apply shading:

- Select the heading.

- Click the **Center** button to centre the text.

- Change the font size to **16pt**.

- Click the **Tables and Borders** button to open the Tables and Borders toolbar.

- If the mouse pointer changes to a pen, press **Esc** to change it back to the normal pointer.

- Click the downward-pointing arrow of the **Shading Color** button and choose **Gray - 50%**.

- Click anywhere on the document to remove the selection highlight.

Note that this shading does not make the heading particularly legible. Try adding coloured shading instead:

- Position the insertion point anywhere in the heading.

- Open the **Format** menu and choose **Borders and Shading.**

- If necessary, click the **Shading** tab to show those options.

- In the Fill list, choose **Yellow.**

- In the Patterns options, open the Style list box and choose **50%.**

- In the Patterns options, open the Color list box and choose **Turquoise.**

The colour of the shading is shown in the Preview box.

- Click **OK** to return to the document.

The heading is now centred and shaded in light green. Now add a red, shadowed border to the second paragraph:

- Select the whole of the second paragraph, headed Hours of Work.

- Open the **Format** menu and choose **Borders and Shading.**

- Click the **Borders** tab to show those options.

- In the Setting group of options, choose **Shadow.**

- In the Style box, make sure the first line style is chosen.

- Open the Width list box and choose the 2¼ **pt** line width.

- If necessary, open the Color list box and choose **Red.**

- Click **OK,** or press **Enter.**

- Click anywhere on the document to remove the selection highlight.

```
Hours of Work:
Monday to Thursday 08:30 to 17:30 with 1 hour lunch
Friday 08:30 to 16:30 with 1 hour lunch
```

Now add a border to the last paragraph, using the Tables and Borders toolbar.

● Select the whole of the last paragraph, starting In return the Employer.

● Open the **Line Style** list box and choose the first double line style.

● If necessary, open the **Line Weight** list box and choose **1 ½ pt**.

 ● Click the downward-pointing arrow of the **Borders** button and then click the **Outside Border** button.

The paragraph is now bordered with a double line.

● Click anywhere on the document to remove the selection highlight.

```
In return the Employer offers the following benefits:
Ten percent of basic salary will be contributed by the Employer, into a private pension scheme.
A company discount card is available for use at selected local establishments.
```

You can now save the document.

● Save the document on your exercise diskette with the filename **a:Ex02a**.

● Print the document if you wish.

 ● Click the **Tables and Borders** button to close the Tables and Borders toolbar.

● Close the document (**File, Close**).

Summary ~ Borders & Shading

To add simple borders to a paragraph:

🖑 Click anywhere in the paragraph around which you wish to place the border

↳   Click the downward-pointing arrow of the **Borders** button in the Formatting toolbar

↳   Click the button which represents the border position you require, e.g., **Top**, **Bottom**, **Left**, **Right**, **Inside** or **Outside**

Using the Tables and Borders toolbar

To display the Tables and Borders toolbar, click the **Tables and Borders** button in the Standard toolbar.

Adding borders to paragraphs

To use the Tables and Borders toolbar to add a border to a paragraph:

↳   Position the insertion point anywhere in the paragraph

↳   Open the **Line Style** list box and choose the line style you require

↳   Click the downward-pointing arrow of the **Borders** button, then click the appropriate border button - **Top**, **Bottom**, **Left**, **Right**, **Inside** or **Outside**

Remove a border by clicking the **No Border** button.

Background shading

To add background shading to a paragraph or heading:

↳   Position the insertion point anywhere in the paragraph

↳   Click the **Shading Color** button in the Tables and Borders toolbar, and choose the shading or colour you require

Using the Borders and Shading dialog box

To apply other border and shading options, use the Borders and Shading dialog box:

✎   Open the **Format** menu and choose **Borders and Shading**

You can then choose a border style, line style and colour for the border. You can also add borders to your page, and can choose a fill colour and pattern for your selection.

Notes

Use this page to make notes of your own.

Page #   Notes

_____   _____

_____   _____

_____   _____

_____   _____

_____   _____

_____   _____

_____   _____

_____   _____

_____   _____

_____   _____

_____   _____

_____   _____

_____   _____

_____   _____

Notes

Use this page to make notes of your own.

Page #   Notes

_____ _____

_____ _____

_____ _____

_____ _____

_____ _____

_____ _____

_____ _____

_____ _____

_____ _____

_____ _____

_____ _____

_____ _____

_____ _____

_____ _____

_____ _____

_____ _____

Chapter 3 ~ More about Tables

Word has a Table feature that will help you create tables quickly and easily. The basic skills for creating tables were covered in the *Microsoft Word 97 Intermediate Course*. This chapter briefly revises these skills, before covering other useful features.

In this chapter you will learn about:

- Drawing a table
- Inserting text before a table
- Using formulae
- Inserting rows and columns
- Merging cells
- Deleting cells
- Removing and adding borders around a table
- Showing and hiding grid lines
- Using AutoFormat on a table
- Cell height and width
- Converting a table to text

The following assumptions are made:

- You know how to format selected text
- You know the basics about borders

To get started

- If necessary, start your Word program.

- If the Office Assistant is displayed at any time throughout this chapter, you should read what it has to say and then close it – click the **Close** button in the Office Assistant window.

You should be starting with a new blank document.

- If necessary, click the **New** button.

Creating a table

You can insert a new table at the insertion point by any of the following methods:

- Click the **Insert Table** button and drag out the number of rows and columns required

- Open the **Table** menu and choose **Insert Table**, and then choose the number of rows and columns required

- Click the **Tables and Borders** button, and then use the mouse to draw the lines for your table

- Open the **Table** menu and choose **Draw Table**, and then use the mouse to draw the lines for your table

- Right-click your document and choose **Draw Table**, and then use the mouse to draw the lines for your table

The **Insert Table** method was covered in the *Microsoft Word 97 Intermediate Course*, so you will be concentrating on using the **Draw Table** feature here.

You will start this chapter by creating a table to report the quarterly sales figures for three items. There will be six rows and six columns.

- Open the **Table** menu and choose **Draw Table**, or click the **Tables and Borders** button in the Standard toolbar, or right-click the empty document and choose **Draw Table**.

The Tables and Borders toolbar is now displayed, and your mouse pointer changes to a small pen. The Office Assistant may also appear at this point, giving advice on drawing tables. You should read what it has to say, then close it.

- If necessary, close the Office Assistant – click the **Close** button in the Office Assistant window.

You have to start by checking the line options in the Tables and Borders toolbar. You will be creating a table with a ½ pt single line border.

- In the Tables and Borders toolbar, open the **Line Style** list box and choose the first line style.

- Open the **Line Weight** list box and choose ½ **pt**.

- Click the **Border Color** button and choose **Automatic**.

You have to start drawing your table, by dragging out a rectangle which will represent the outside border for the table. It needs to be approximately 15cm wide by 6cm high (6" x 3"). You may wish to display the ruler to assist you.

- If required, open the **View** menu and choose **Ruler**.

You can now start to draw your table.

- Click towards the top left-hand corner of your page, and drag the mouse down and to the right until you have dragged out a table approx. **15**cm wide by **6**cm high (**6" wide x 3" high**).

Your table should resemble the following picture.

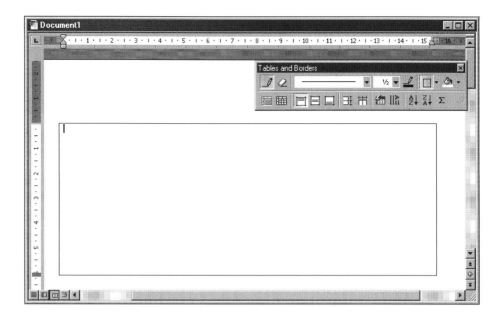

You can now add the lines to the table.

●   Using the mouse, draw a horizontal line
through the centre of the rectangle - click
the centre of the left-hand border and drag
the mouse to the right.

Your table should now be split into two rows. Next, try
splitting the table vertically.

●   Click the centre of the top border and drag
the mouse through the centre line to the
bottom border.

Your table should now be made up of four rectangles.

- Continue to draw lines in the same manner, to create the table as shown in the following picture:

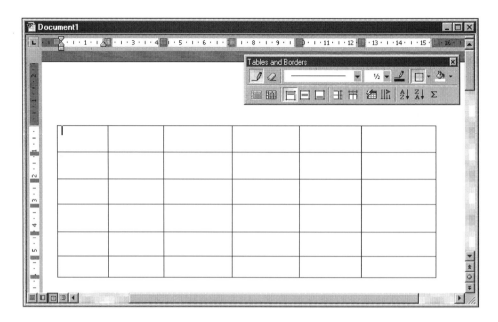

✎ If you make any mistakes, click the **Eraser** button in the Tables and Borders toolbar, and erase the incorrect line before drawing it again

Your empty table should now have six columns and six rows.

- Click the **Draw Table** button, or press **Esc**, to return to the normal mouse pointer.

You can now add a title above the table.

Inserting text before a table

As the document starts off with the table, you can't just position the insertion point before it.

- Position the mouse pointer at the beginning of the first cell, and then press **Enter**.

You now have an empty line where you can type the heading.

- Type:

  Quarterly Sales Figures - Marine Division - 1996/7

You can now centre the heading and format it as 16pt, bold and underlined.

- Format the heading as **16pt, bold** and **underlined,** and centre it.

- Press **Enter** to create an extra blank line before the table.

You are now ready to enter some figures into the table.

Filling in the table

To move between the cells, you can simply click the desired cell, or use the ←→↑↓ keys or the **Tab** key.

- Using a font size of **10pt,** type the details shown below:

Marine Division					
Product line	First Quarter	Second Quarter	Third Quarter	Fourth Quarter	Totals
Masts	450	1050	300	600	
Sails	1440	2553	1027	2031	
Hulls	5614	10880	2004	4786	
Totals					

Save the table

Now save the table on your exercise diskette.

- Make sure your exercise diskette is in drive A.

- Open the **File** menu and choose **Save,** or click the **Save** button, or press **Ctrl+S.**

The Save As dialog box is displayed.

- In the File name box, type:

    a:My Table

- Click **Save,** or press **Enter.**

Using formulae

So far in your table, you have not added up the different totals. You do not need to do this manually; you can use Word's Formula function to help you. Try calculating the sum of the first row of figures as follows:

- Move to the last cell in the Masts row.

- Open the **Table** menu and choose **Formula.**

The Formula dialog box is opened.

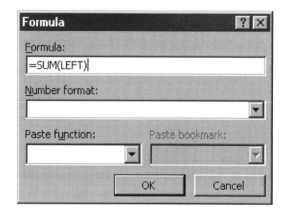

The Formula box suggests that Word should calculate the sum of all the figures to the left of the cell, using the formula =SUM(LEFT). This is exactly what you want to do.

- Click **OK** to confirm the suggested formula.

The total, 2400, is filled in automatically. Now you will try changing a value in the first row.

- Change the first value in the Masts row from 450 to **475.**

Note that the row total is not updated.

If you change any of the values in the row, the total is not recalculated automatically.

- Move to the last cell in the Masts row, then open the **Table** menu and choose **Formula** again.

The Formula dialog box is opened again.

- Click **OK** to confirm the suggested formula.

The row total is now updated to 2425.

Filling in the next row total

Now you will repeat the above instructions to fill in the next row total.

- Move to the last cell in the Sails row.

- Open the **Table** menu and choose **Formula** again.

The Formula dialog box is opened. This time Word suggests the formula =SUM(ABOVE). This is wrong - you need the sum of the figures to the left of the cell.

- Change the formula to:

  =SUM(LEFT)

- Click **OK** to confirm the suggested formula.

The Sails row total is now calculated as 7051.

The Repeat feature

Word has a **Repeat** option in the **Edit** menu, which often allows you to repeat the previous operation on another cell or selected text. You can use this feature to calculate the Hulls row total.

- Move to the last cell in the Hulls row.

- Open the **Edit** menu and choose **Repeat Formula,** or just press **Ctrl+Y**.

The Hulls row total is calculated as 23284.

Calculating the column totals

The next step is to calculate the column totals. You can do this by using the Formula dialog box in the same way as above, or you can use the **AutoSum** button in the Tables and Borders toolbar. This time you will use the **AutoSum** button.

- Move to the last cell in the First Quarter column.

- Click the **AutoSum** button in the Tables and Border toolbar.

The First Quarter column total is calculated as 7529.

- Move to the last cell in the Second Quarter column.

- Click the **AutoSum** button.

- Move to the last cell in the Third Quarter column and click the **AutoSum** button.

- Move to the last cell in the Fourth Quarter column and click the **AutoSum** button.

- Finally, move to the last cell in the Totals column and click the **AutoSum** button.

Your table should resemble the following picture.

Quarterly Sales Figures – Marine Division – 1996/7

Marine Division					
Product line	First Quarter	Second Quarter	Third Quarter	Fourth Quarter	Totals
Masts	475	1050	300	600	2425
Sails	1440	2553	1027	2031	7051
Hulls	5614	10880	2004	4786	23234
Totals	7529	14483	3331	7417	32760

- Click the **Save** button, or press **Ctrl+S**, to save the document changes.

Simple formatting

You can now format the table.

- Make the whole of the first column of the table **bold**.

- Make the whole of the second row of the table, excluding the first entry (which is already bold), **bold** and **right-aligned**.

- **Right-align** all the cells containing numbers.

You can also align the text vertically within the cells.

- Open the **Table** menu and choose **Select Table**, to select all the cells in the table.

- Click the **Center Vertically** button in the Tables and Borders toolbar.

- Click any cell in the table to remove the selection highlight.

AutoFit column widths

The **AutoFit** option adjusts the width of selected columns in the table to fit the largest entry in each column. You need to select the whole table to do this.

- Click anywhere on the table, then open the **Table** menu and choose **Select Table**.

- Open the **Table** menu and choose **Cell Height and Width**.

The Cell Height and Width dialog box is displayed. There are two sets of options: **Row** and **Column**.

- Click the **Column** tab to show those options.

- Click the **AutoFit** button.

The columns are adjusted automatically.

Inserting a new row

You will now change the table by inserting a new row above the column headings and then joining some cells together. The next picture will give you an idea of what you are trying to achieve.

Quarterly Sales Figures – Marine Division – 1996/7

Marine Division					
	Confirmed			Estimated	
Product line	First Quarter	Second Quarter	Third Quarter	Fourth Quarter	Totals
Masts	475	1050	300	600	2425
Sails	1440	2553	1027	2031	7051
Hulls	5614	10880	2004	4786	23284
Totals	7529	14483	3331	7417	32760

When you use the **Insert** option in the **Table** menu, or in the shortcut menu, it will change according to what is currently selected.

🖑   If you have a complete row selected, the menu option will be **Insert Rows** and you will only be able to insert a complete row

🖑   If you have a complete column selected, the menu option will be **Insert Columns** and you will only be able to insert a complete column

🖑   If you have just a cell selected, the menu option will be **Insert Cells**, but a dialog box will give you the option of inserting a whole row or column

---

✑   *If you select a number of rows or columns, Word will insert that number of rows or columns above/before the selected rows/columns.*

Start by inserting a row above the column headings.

●   `Select the row of headings in the table starting` Product line.

- Right-click the selection and choose **Insert Rows**.

You now have a new empty row above the column headings.

Merging cells

Sometimes you can select two or more cells and merge them into one larger cell. This is what you need to do now.

- Select the whole of the first row of the table.

- Open the **Table** menu and choose **Merge Cells**, or click the **Merge Cells** button in the Tables and Borders toolbar.

Now there is only one cell across the top of the table. You should now centre the heading.

- Click the **Center** button, or press **Ctrl+E**, to centre the text.

You will now add the Confirmed and Estimated headings.

- Select the second, third and fourth cells in the second row of the table.

- Open the **Table** menu and choose **Merge Cells**, or click the **Merge Cells** button.

The three cells are merged into one.

- Type:

  Confirmed

- Click the **Center** button, or press **Ctrl+E**, to centre the text.

- Press the → key to move to the next cell.

- Type:

  Estimated

- Click the **Center** button, or press **Ctrl+E**, to centre the text.

Word doesn't always let you merge cells. Try this:

●   `Select the first two cells in the first column.`

●   `Open the `**`Table`**` menu and choose `**`Merge Cells`**` - no, you can't! The option is 'greyed out' and not available.`

Removing and adding borders

By default, Word will place a ½ pt line border around the cells of your tables. You can remove or change the border as you wish. Try removing the border lines now:

●   `Open the `**`Table`**` menu and choose `**`Select Table`**`.`

●   `Click the downward-pointing arrow of the `**`Borders`**` highlight. button, and then click the `**`No Border`**` button.`

●   `Click anywhere on the table to remove the selection`

Your table no longer has borders.

Displaying and hiding the grid lines

Sometimes you may find it useful to display grid lines that can be used to guide you when working with tables. You may already see faint grid lines surrounding your table. Grid lines are not printed when you print your document.

●   `If the faint grid lines are not currently displayed, open the `**`Table`**` menu and choose `**`Show Gridlines`**`.`

Faint grey lines are displayed, indicating the borders of the cells. You can now hide the gridlines.

●   `Open the `**`Table`**` menu and choose `**`Hide Gridlines`**`.`

The grid lines are hidden.

Adding borders to the table

Finally, you can add borders to the table using either the Borders toolbar, or the Borders and Shading dialog box. This time you can try the dialog box.

- Select the whole table.

- Open the **Format** menu and choose **Borders and Shading**.

The Borders and Shading dialog box is displayed.

- If necessary, click the **Borders** tab to show those options.

- In the Setting group of options, choose **Grid**.

- In the Style list make sure the first line style is chosen.

- Open the Width list box and choose **1 pt**.

- Open the Color list box and choose **Auto**.

- Click **OK**.

- Click anywhere on the document to remove the selection highlight.

The table now has a 1 pt line border. Now try placing a double-lined border around the outside of the table, using the Tables and Borders toolbar.

- Select the whole table.

- In the Tables and Borders toolbar, open the **Line Style** list box and choose the first double-line style.

- Click the downward-pointing arrow of the **Border** button, and then click the **Outside Border** button.

- Click anywhere on the table to remove the selection highlight.

Your table should now resemble the sample table. You can now save and print the document.

- Save your document, then print it if you wish.

Deleting cells, rows or columns

Sometimes, you may wish to delete specific cells, rows or columns from a table. As with the **Insert** option, the exact wording of the **Delete** option depends on what is currently selected. Deletions can be done in two ways. First, select the cells, rows or columns to be deleted. Then do one of the following:

    ✍   Open the **Table** menu and choose **Delete Cells/ Rows/Columns**

    ✍   Right-click the selection and choose **Delete Cells/ Rows/Columns** in the shortcut menu

If you have selected *cells* for deletion, Word will display a dialog box giving you various options. Try this out now by deleting the second row.

- Select the first cell in the second row.

- Right-click the selection and choose **Delete Cells**.

The Delete Cells dialog box is displayed.

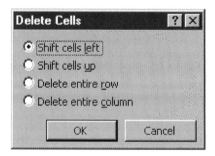

You have to be careful which option you choose because this single merged cell is part of the first column of the table.

    ✍   If you choose **Shift cells left**, the cell will be deleted and the rest of the row will move over.

    ✍   If you choose **Shift cells up**, all the other cells in the first column will be moved upwards. The row headings will then be mis-aligned.

    ✍   If you choose **Delete entire row**, the row will be deleted, leaving the rest of the table unchanged.

↳   If you choose **Delete entire column**, the whole of the first column will be deleted, removing all the row headings, as well as the Marine Division heading.

In this particular instance you need to delete the entire row.

- Click the **Delete entire row** option so that it is chosen.

- Click OK, or press Enter.

The second row of the table is deleted.

On your own

If you want, you can undo the deletion and investigate the effect of choosing the other options in the Delete Cells dialog box.

- If you wish, undo the deletion (**Edit, Undo**) and investigate the other options in the Delete Cells dialog box.

Finally, when you are ready, you can close the document.

- Open the **File** menu and choose **Close** – choose **Yes** to save the changes.

You can also close the Tables and Borders toolbar.

- Click the **Tables and Borders** button in the Standard toolbar, to close the Tables and Borders toolbar.

Table AutoFormat

Word has an AutoFormat feature that lets you choose one of many pre-programmed formats.

If you have a table you wish to format, you should click the table to make it active, and then do one of the following:

↳   Open the **Table** menu and choose **Table AutoFormat**

↳   Right-click the table and choose **Table AutoFormat** in the shortcut menu

If you want to create a table and choose its format at the same time:

↳   Open the **Table** menu and choose **Insert Table** to open the Insert Table dialog box

↳   Choose the number of rows and columns you require

↳   Click the **AutoFormat** button

As you need to create another table, you will use this last method here. First you need to open a new blank document.

- Click the **New** button.

- Open the **Table** menu and choose **Insert Table**.

The Insert Table dialog box is displayed.

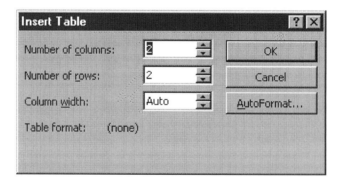

- Change the current entry in the <u>Number of columns</u> box to **5**.

- Change the current entry in the <u>Number of rows</u> box to **4**.

- Click the **AutoFormat** button.

The Table AutoFormat dialog box is displayed.

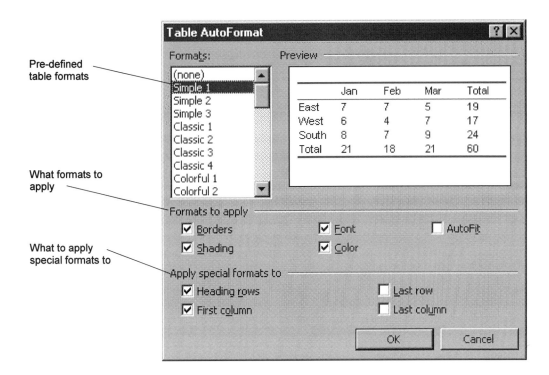

Pre-defined table formats

What formats to apply

What to apply special formats to

Basically there are three things to choose:

🐍 A pre-defined format can be chosen in the Formats box.

🐍 The formats can be applied to various components of the table; these components are chosen in the Formats to apply group of options. The **AutoFit** option, if ticked, will change the column widths of your table automatically, to fit the contents of the column.

🐍 Different formats can be applied to row and column headings, etc., to make them stand out. You can choose which parts to apply a different format to by choosing the various Apply special formats to options.

The Preview box always shows you an example of the table using the options you have chosen.

● In the Formats list, choose the **Columns 3** option.

● In the Formats to apply group of options, click **Shading** so that it is not ticked.

Note the difference this makes to the example in the Preview box.

- Click the **Shading** option again so that it is ticked.

- In the Formats to apply group of options, click the **Color** option so that it is not ticked.

Again, note the difference in the Preview box.

- In the Apply special formats to group of options, click **Last row** so that it is ticked.

- Click the **First column** option so that it is not ticked.

- Click **OK** to close the Table AutoFormat dialog box.

- Click **OK** to close the Insert Table dialog box.

The table is inserted into your document and formatted accordingly.

- On your own, fill in a few imaginary figures.

Changing the AutoFormat

You can now try changing the format of your table using the AutoFormat feature.

- Right-click anywhere in your table and choose **Table AutoFormat** in the shortcut menu.

The Table AutoFormat dialog box is displayed again.

- On your own, try out a few of the other formats on your table.

- When you are ready, open the **File** menu and choose **Close** – don't save the changes.

Cell height and width

Within the table, the height of each row and the width of each column can be adjusted. To investigate this you need to open the **European Populations** document from your exercise diskette.

- Open the document **European Populations** from your exercise diskette.

You will now adjust the column widths in this table. This can be done using the mouse to drag the column border out or in, or more precisely using the Cell Height and Width dialog box. You could also use the **AutoFit** option covered earlier in this chapter.

> *You have to be very careful adjusting the table because individual cells can be changed as well as whole columns or rows, giving some strange effects. If you make a change you don't want, use the Undo feature immediately afterwards to undo the change.*

Using the mouse to adjust the column width

Use the mouse to adjust the width of the first column:

- Position the mouse pointer over the border of the right-hand edge of the first column – it will change to a double-headed arrow.

- Drag the border to the left until the column is just wide enough for the entry Luxembourg.

Using the Cell Height and Width dialog box

Now make the second, third and fourth columns 2.5 cm (or 1") wide using the Cell Height and Width dialog box. To open the Cell Height and Width dialog box:

- Select the desired rows or columns (or select the whole table)

✎ Open the **Table** menu and choose **Cell Height and Width**

Try it now, just selecting columns 2 to 4:

● Select columns 2 to 4.

● Open the **Table** menu and choose **Cell Height and Width**.

The Cell Height and Width dialog box is displayed. There are two sets of options: **Row** and **Column**.

● If necessary, click the **Column** tab to show those options.

Check here to see
which columns are
selected

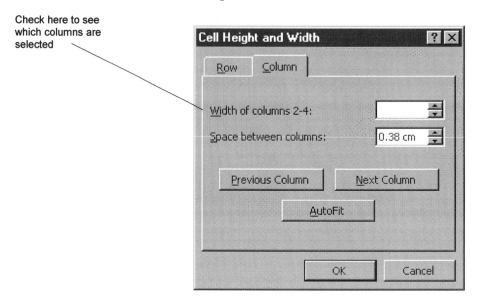

You can change the width of the selected column(s) and the space between columns.

● In the Width of columns 2-4 box, type:

(or **1**, if you are using inches)

Row height options

You can now check the row options.

● Click the **Row** tab to show those options.

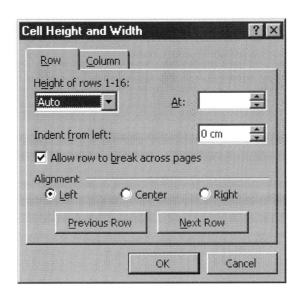

The **Row** options let you adjust the row height. This is normally set to **Auto**. This means that it will adjust automatically according to the font size used. The **Previous Row** and **Next Row** buttons let you swap rows to format other rows without first closing the dialog box. The Alignment options let you choose whether to align your table to the left or right margins, or to centre it. Try centring the table on the page:

- In the Alignment set of options, click **Center** so that it is chosen.

You can accept the other settings as they are.

- Click **OK**, or press **Enter**.

The column widths are adjusted. Finish off by right-aligning the last three columns - they should already be selected - and centre the table heading.

- With columns 2 to 4 selected, click the **Align Right** button, or press **Ctrl+R**.

- Centre the heading, European Populations.

- Click anywhere on the document, below the table, to remove the selection highlight.

European Populations

Country	Area	Population	Density
Austria	32,374	7,700,000	238
Belgium	11,781	9,885,000	839
Denmark	17,170	5,200,000	302
Finland	130,129	4,970,000	38
France	211,208	56,300,000	267
Germany	137,744	77,750,000	564
Greece	50,944	10,200,000	200
Holland	15,770	15,000,000	951
Ireland	27,137	3,510,000	129
Italy	116,304	57,500,000	494
Luxembourg	998	377,000	378
Portugal	35,553	10,435,000	294
Spain	194,897	39,300,000	202
Sweden	173,732	8,525,000	49
UK	94,247	57,500,000	610

Converting a table to text

The last section in this chapter covers converting a table to text. When you do so, the cells in each row are separated by a character that you choose.

- Select the table - click anywhere in the table, then open the **Table** menu and choose **Select Table**.

- Open the **Table** menu and choose **Convert Table to Text**.

The Convert Table To Text dialog box is displayed.

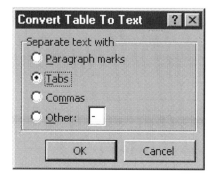

If you choose the **Tabs** option, the table will still look like a table after the conversion. You could use a completely different character, say the exclamation mark. Try this now:

- Click Other so that it is chosen, and type:

      !

- Click **OK**, or press **Enter**.

The table is converted to normal text with ! separating the entries.

Ending the session

You have now completed the tutorial in this chapter. There is an additional exercise that you may wish to do before moving on to the next chapter or exiting Word. First, you should close the current document.

- Open the **File** menu and choose **Close** - choose **No** to avoid saving the changes.

- If you are not continuing directly with the extra exercise or the next chapter and want to stop now, open the **File** menu and choose **Exit** to exit Word.

Exercise 3a

- Create the table as shown below and format it.

Working Parents 1992

Age of youngest child	Parents working		Absence from work (%)	
	Women	*Men*	*Women*	*Men*
0 - 2 years	77	89	51	14
3 - 6 years	86	93	16	11
7 - 10 years	89	94	14	10
11-16 years	91	93	14	10

Source: Work force investigation, Sweden.

- When you are ready, save the document on your exercise diskette with the filename **a:Ex03a**.

- Print the document, or use Print Preview just to view it.

- Close the Tables and Border toolbar, then close the document (**File, Close**).

Summary ~ More about Tables

Creating a table

To create a table, you can do any of the following:

- ✎ Click the **Insert Table** button and drag out the number of rows and columns required

- ✎ Open the **Table** menu and choose **Insert Table**, and then choose the number of rows and columns required

- ✎ Click the **Tables and Borders** button, and then use the mouse to draw the lines for your table

- ✎ Open the **Table** menu and choose **Draw Table**, and then use the mouse to draw the lines for your table

- ✎ Right-click your document and choose **Draw Table**, and then use the mouse to draw the lines for your table

To insert text before a table, position the insertion point in the first cell of the table and press **Enter**.

Using formulae

- ✎ Position the insertion point in the last cell of the column or row you want to total

- ✎ Open the **Table** menu and choose **Formula**

- ✎ Modify the suggested formula if necessary

To repeat a formula in an adjacent cell, use **Edit**, **Redo**, or press **Ctrl+Y**.

Σ

↳ You can also position the insertion point in the last cell of the column or row you want to total, and then click the **AutoSum** button

Inserting rows or columns

To insert a row/column:

↳ Select the row or column above/before which you want to insert the row/column

↳ Right-click the selection and choose **Insert Row/Column**

Deleting rows or columns

↳ Select the row(s) or column(s) you want to delete

↳ Right-click the selection and choose **Delete Row/Column**

Merging cells

↳ Select the cells you wish to merge

↳ Open the **Table** menu and choose **Merge Cells**, or click the **Merge Cells** button in the Tables and Borders toolbar

Removing borders from a table

By default, Word will place a ½ pt border around all the cells in your table. To remove these lines from a table.

↳ Select the table

↳ Click the downward-pointing arrow in the **Borders** button, and then click the **No Border** button

Once you have removed the borders, you may wish to display grid lines that guide you when editing your document. To do this, open the **Table** menu and choose **Show Gridlines**. These faint grid lines are not printed.

Table AutoFormat

↪   Right-click the table and choose **Table AutoFormat**

↪   Decide which formats to apply - borders, shading, colour, etc.

↪   Decide whether to apply special formats to specific components of the table

Changing the column width

To open the Cell Height and Width dialog box, open the **Table** menu and choose **Cell Height and Width**. Click the **Column** tab then set the exact value you require, or use the **AutoFit** button.

Row height and table alignment

The Row height is adjusted automatically to accommodate the chosen font size. Manual adjustments can be made in the Cell Height and Width dialog box. To align the table to left, centre or right, choose one of the Alignment options in the Cell Height and Width dialog box (**Row** tab).

Changing a table to text

First select the table, then open the **Table** menu and choose **Convert Table to Text**. Choose the character with which you want to separate the text.

Notes

Use this page to make notes of your own.

Page #   Notes

_____   _____

_____   _____

_____   _____

_____   _____

_____   _____

_____   _____

_____   _____

_____   _____

_____   _____

_____   _____

_____   _____

_____   _____

_____   _____

_____   _____

Notes

Use this page to make notes of your own.

Page #   Notes

_____   _____

_____   _____

_____   _____

_____   _____

_____   _____

_____   _____

_____   _____

_____   _____

_____   _____

_____   _____

_____   _____

_____   _____

_____   _____

_____   _____

_____   _____

Chapter 4 ~ Sorting

Once you have created a list or a glossary in a document, you may need to sort it in a specific order: alphabetically or numerically. This can be achieved using the **Table**, **Sort** menu option.

In this chapter you will learn about:

- ✎ Sorting a table
- ✎ Sort options
- ✎ Multiple sort criteria
- ✎ Sorting paragraphs

To get started

- If necessary, start your Word program.

- If the Office Assistant is displayed at any time throughout this chapter, you should read what it has to say and then close it – click the **Close** button in the Office Assistant window.

- Open the **Sorting** document from your exercise diskette.

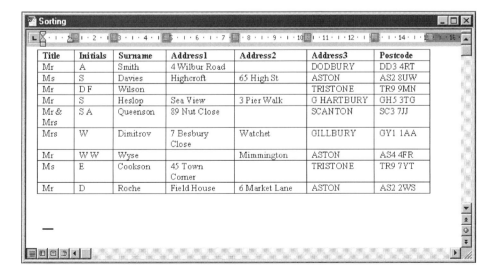

Title	Initials	Surname	Address1	Address2	Address3	Postcode
Mr	A	Smith	4 Wilbur Road		DODBURY	DD3 4RT
Ms	S	Davies	Highcroft	65 High St	ASTON	AS2 8UW
Mr	D F	Wilson			TRISTONE	TR9 9MN
Mr	S	Heslop	Sea View	3 Pier Walk	G HARTBURY	GH5 3TG
Mr & Mrs	S A	Queenson	89 Nut Close		SCANTON	SC3 7JJ
Mrs	W	Dimitrov	7 Besbury Close	Watchet	GILLBURY	GY1 1AA
Mr	W W	Wyse		Mimmington	ASTON	AS4 4FR
Ms	E	Cookson	45 Town Corner		TRISTONE	TR9 7YT
Mr	D	Roche	Field House	6 Market Lane	ASTON	AS2 2WS

You can ignore any spelling errors that Word may identify with a wavy red line.

Sorting a table

You can sort a whole table, or limit the sort to selected rows.

● Click anywhere on the table.

● Open the **Table** menu and choose **Sort**.

The Sort dialog box is displayed.

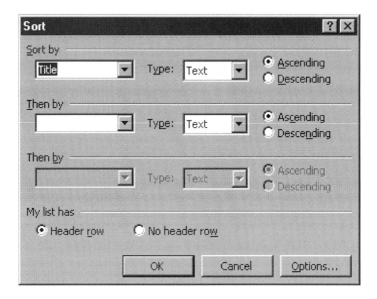

You can choose which column(s) to sort by, the type of sort and the order. Notice that there is a <u>My list has</u> group of options that allows you to say whether or not your selection includes a header row. If there is one, you will not normally want to include it in the sort.

● If necessary, in the <u>My list has</u> group of options, click **Header row** so that it is chosen.

Assume you want to sort the table in postcode order.

● Open the <u>Sort by</u> list box and choose **Postcode**.

● Make sure the <u>Type</u> option is set to **Text**.

● Make sure the **Ascending** option is chosen.

- Click **OK**.

- Click anywhere on the document to remove the selection highlight.

The table should now be in alphabetical order, according to the postcodes.

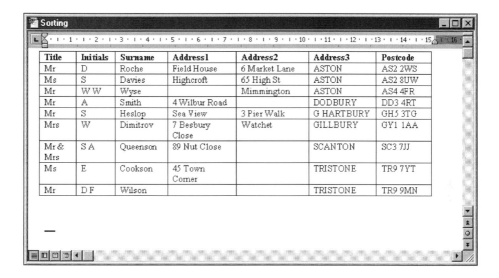

Title	Initials	Surname	Address1	Address2	Address3	Postcode
Mr	D	Roche	Field House	6 Market Lane	ASTON	AS2 2WS
Ms	S	Davies	Highcroft	65 High St	ASTON	AS2 8UW
Mr	W W	Wyse		Mimmington	ASTON	AS4 4FR
Mr	A	Smith	4 Wilbur Road		DODBURY	DD3 4RT
Mr	S	Heslop	Sea View	3 Pier Walk	G HARTBURY	GH5 3TG
Mrs	W	Dimitrov	7 Besbury Close	Watchet	GILLBURY	GY1 1AA
Mr & Mrs	S A	Queenson	89 Nut Close		SCANTON	SC3 7JJ
Ms	E	Cookson	45 Town Corner		TRISTONE	TR9 7YT
Mr	D F	Wilson			TRISTONE	TR9 9MN

Sort options

Each time you open the Sort dialog box, you can make several changes to control the sort.

- Click anywhere on the table.

- Open the **Table** menu and choose **Sort**.

The Sort dialog box is displayed again. The following options are available:

- **Sort by** - allows you to choose which column to use for your primary sort within the table

- **Then by** - allows you to choose a second or third column to sort by

- **Type** - allows you to choose the type of data that is used in the chosen column, e.g., text, number, or a date

- **Ascending/Descending** - allows you to choose the order in which you want to sort the table

The **Options** button gives you further choices.

●   Click the **Options** button.

The Sort Options dialog box is displayed.

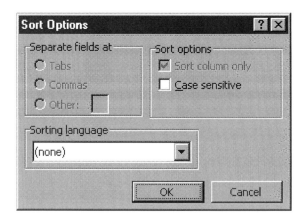

    ✎   **Case sensitive** - when ticked, will sort words with identical letters according to whether they are lower case, capitalised or upper case (e.g., in ascending order: charlie, Charlie, CHARLIE).

    ✎   **Sort column only** - allows you to sort a column without sorting the remaining cells in the rows. This option is only available if you have selected a particular column for sorting before opening the Sort dialog box. In most cases, however, you will want all the information in one row to be kept together, even if you are sorting by one of the columns.

    ✎   The **Separate fields at** option is available when you are sorting by paragraphs.

●   Click **Cancel,** or press **Esc,** to close the Sort Options dialog box.

●   Click **Cancel,** or press **Esc,** to close the Sort dialog box.

Using multiple sort criteria

Assume you want to sort the table with all the men, (Mr) first in surname order, followed by all the women (Mrs, Ms) in surname order. To do this, you need to set the title column as the first sort column, then the surname column as the second.

●   Click anywhere on the table.

●   Open the **Table** menu and choose **Sort**.

The Sort dialog box is displayed. You will start by setting the details for the first sort column.

●   If necessary, in the <u>My list has</u> group of options, click **Header row** so that it is chosen.

●   Open the <u>Sort by</u> list box and choose **Title**.

●   Make sure the <u>Type</u> option is set to **Text**.

●   Make sure the **Ascending** option is chosen.

Next, you will set the details for the second sort column.

●   Open the first <u>Then by</u> list box and choose **Surname**.

●   Make sure the <u>Type</u> option is set to **Text**.

●   Make sure the **Ascending** option is chosen.

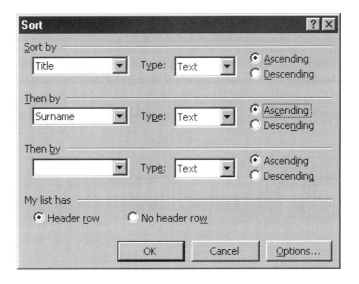

●   Click **OK**.

- Click anywhere on the document to remove the selection highlight.

The table should now be sorted, as shown in the next picture.

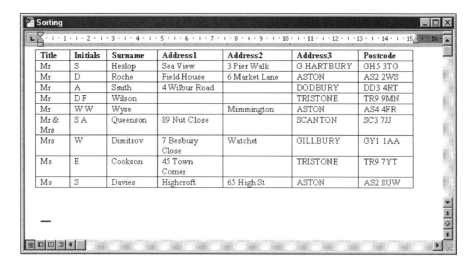

Title	Initials	Surname	Address1	Address2	Address3	Postcode
Mr	S	Heslop	Sea View	3 Pier Walk	G HARTBURY	GH5 3TG
Mr	D	Roche	Field House	6 Market Lane	ASTON	AS2 2WS
Mr	A	Smith	4 Wilbur Road		DODBURY	DD3 4RT
Mr	D F	Wilson			TRISTONE	TR9 9MN
Mr	W W	Wyse		Mimmington	ASTON	AS4 4FR
Mr & Mrs	S A	Queenson	89 Nut Close		SCANTON	SC3 7JJ
Mrs	W	Dimitrov	7 Besbury Close	Watchet	GILLBURY	GY1 1AA
Ms	E	Cookson	45 Town Corner		TRISTONE	TR9 7YT
Ms	S	Davies	Highcroft	65 High St	ASTON	AS2 8UW

Finish off by closing the document.

- Open the **File** menu and choose **Close** – do not save the changes.

Sorting paragraphs

Paragraphs can be sorted in the same way.

- Open the **Technical Terms** document from your exercise diskette.

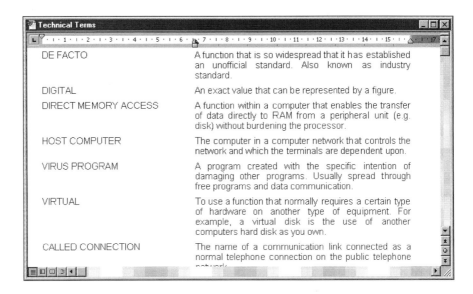

Study the document to see that the paragraphs are not sorted.

● Select the entire document (**Ctrl+A**).

● Open the **Table** menu and choose **Sort**.

The Sort Text dialog box is opened with the same options as the Sort Table dialog box. This time, you will sort the paragraphs in reverse order for a change.

● If necessary, open the <u>Sort by</u> list box and choose **Paragraphs**.

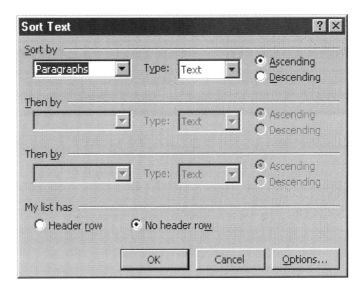

● Click the **Descending** option so that it is chosen.

- Click **OK**.

- Click anywhere on the document to remove the selection highlight.

The document is sorted, rearranging the paragraphs in reverse alphabetical order.

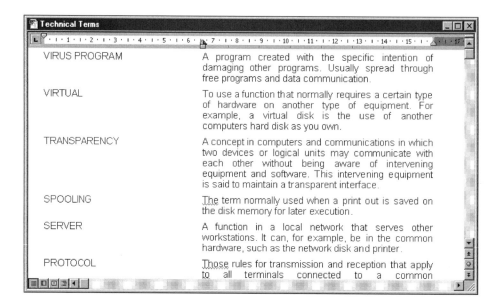

In this particular document, the definition is separated from its description by a tab character.

- Click the **Show/Hide ¶** button to show the tab characters.

If, at another time, a different character is used to separate the fields, you need to tell Word which character to use. To do this:

  ✎ Click **Options** in the Sort Text dialog box

  ✎ In the <u>Separate fields at</u> group of options, choose **Tabs**, **Commas**, or define an **Other** character

You can now hide the tab characters.

- Click the **Show/Hide ¶** button again to hide the tab characters.

Ending the session

You have now completed the tutorial in this chapter. There are two additional exercises that you may wish to do before moving on to the next chapter or exiting Word. First, you should close the current document.

- Open the **File** menu and choose **Close** - choose **No** to avoid saving the changes.

- If you are not continuing directly with the extra exercises or the next chapter and want to stop now, open the **File** menu and choose **Exit** to exit Word.

Exercise 4a

In this exercise you will practise sorting a table of data.

- Open the **Birthdays** document from your exercise diskette.

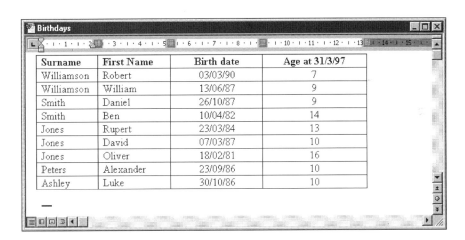

Surname	First Name	Birth date	Age at 31/3/97
Williamson	Robert	03/03/90	7
Williamson	William	13/06/87	9
Smith	Daniel	26/10/87	9
Smith	Ben	10/04/82	14
Jones	Rupert	23/03/84	13
Jones	David	07/03/87	10
Jones	Oliver	18/02/81	16
Peters	Alexander	23/09/86	10
Ashley	Luke	30/10/86	10

You can start by sorting the children according to their first names.

- Click anywhere on the table.

- Open the **Table** menu and choose **Sort**.

- Open the **Sort by** list box and choose **First Name**.

- Make sure the **Type** option is set to **Text**.

- Make sure the **Ascending** option is chosen.

- If necessary, in the <u>My list has</u> group of options, click **Header row** so that it is chosen.

- Click **OK**.

The table is sorted with Alexander Peters at the top; William Williamson at the bottom. Now sort by surname and first name.

- Open the **Table** menu and choose **Sort**.

- Open the <u>Sort by</u> list box and choose **Surname**.

- Make sure the <u>Type</u> option is set to **Text**.

- Make sure the **Ascending** option is chosen.

- Open the <u>Then by</u> list box and choose **First Name**.

- Make sure the <u>Type</u> option is set to **Text**.

- Make sure the **Ascending** option is chosen.

- Click **OK**.

- Click anywhere on the document to remove the selection highlight.

The table is sorted with Luke Ashley at the top; William Williamson at the bottom.

- On your own, sort the table by surname (ascending) and age (descending).

The table should start with Luke Ashley and end with Robert Williamson.

- Finally, sort it by birth date (ascending).

The table should now start with Oliver Jones and end with Robert Williamson.

- Close the file without saving the changes.

Exercise 4b

In this exercise you will sort the paragraphs in a glossary into alphabetical order.

- Open the **Glossary** document from your exercise diskette.

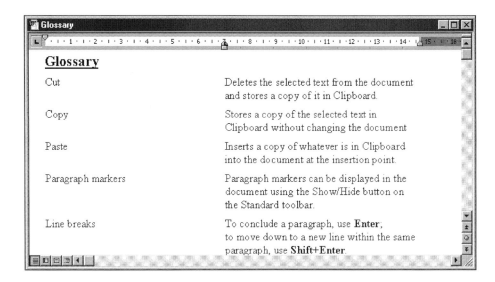

- Select the text, excluding the title.

- Open the **Table** menu and choose **Sort**.

- Open the Sort by box and choose **Paragraphs**.

- Make sure the Type option is set to **Text**.

- Make sure the **Ascending** option is chosen.

- Click **OK**.

- Click anywhere on the document to remove the selection highlight.

The glossary is sorted with Copy at the top and Undo at the bottom.

- When you are ready, close the document without saving the changes.

Summary ~ Sorting

To sort a table:

    ☙   Click anywhere on the table

    ☙   Open the **Table** menu and choose **Sort**

    ☙   If your table has a header row, make sure the **Header row** option is chosen

    ☙   In the Sort by list box, choose the column to sort by

Sort options

There are three options for each sort:

    ☙   Sort by/Then by - which column to sort by first, second and third, if required

    ☙   The Type of data you are sorting: **Text**, **Number** or **Date**

    ☙   The order in which to sort the table: **Ascending** or **Descending**

Multiple sort criteria

For a multiple sort:

    ☙   Click anywhere on the table

    ☙   Open the **Table** menu and choose **Sort**

    ☙   If your table has a header row, make sure the **Header row** option is chosen

    ☙   In the Sort by list box, choose the column to sort by

    ☙   In the Then by list box(es), choose the column(s) for the second (and third) sort criteria

    ☙   Set the Type and **Ascending/Descending** options as required

Sorting paragraphs

To sort paragraphs in a document:

      ☙   Select the paragraphs that require sorting

      ☙   Open the **Table** menu and choose **Sort**

      ☙   Set the Type and **Ascending/Descending** options as required

For paragraph sorting, the Sort by box should show **Paragraphs**.

Notes

Use this page to make notes of your own.

Page #   Notes

_____   _____

_____   _____

_____   _____

_____   _____

_____   _____

_____   _____

_____   _____

_____   _____

_____   _____

_____   _____

_____   _____

_____   _____

_____   _____

_____   _____

_____   _____

Chapter 5 ~ Newspaper Columns

Newspaper columns are the familiar style of columns found in a newspaper or newsletter. In this chapter you will learn the basics about columns and column widths.

In this chapter you will learn about:

- Setting the number of columns on a page
- Shrink to fit
- Adding vertical lines between columns
- Adjusting the width of columns and column spacings
- The ruler
- Different columns in the same document

Remember the following:

- When you change the number of columns, if no text is selected, the change is applied to the whole document.
- When you change the number of columns, the change can be applied to selected text only. In this case Word automatically creates a clearly marked 'section' for the selected text.
- If the document already has some sections, and you change the number of columns without selecting any text, the change is applied to the current section only.

To get started

- If necessary, start your Word program.
- Open the **Printers** document from your exercise diskette.

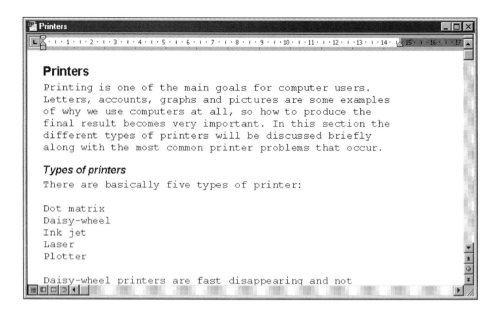

Printers

Printing is one of the main goals for computer users. Letters, accounts, graphs and pictures are some examples of why we use computers at all, so how to produce the final result becomes very important. In this section the different types of printers will be discussed briefly along with the most common printer problems that occur.

Types of printers

There are basically five types of printer:

Dot matrix
Daisy-wheel
Ink jet
Laser
Plotter

Daisy-wheel printers are fast disappearing and not

Changing the number of columns

The number of columns is changed using the **Columns** button, or the Columns dialog box. You will try both. First change the document to have three columns, using the **Columns** button.

● Click the **Columns** button in the Standard toolbar.

A small box is opened beneath the button and you can choose how many columns you want. Click the second column and you get two columns, and so on.

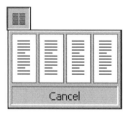

● Click the third column.

The document now has three columns. However, unless you are in the Page Layout view, you will not be able to see the three columns.

- If necessary, switch to the Page Layout view – open the **View** menu and choose **Page Layout,** or click the **Page Layout View** button.

The columns are now visible. You will change the number of columns again later on.

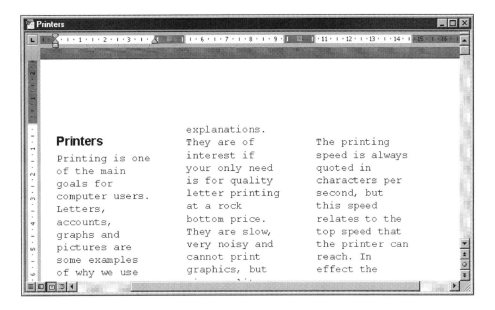

> ✎ *The exact layout of the text on the page will depend on the printer you are using; your second and third columns may start with different words.*

- Press **Page Down/Page Up** to scroll through the pages.

- Press **Ctrl+Home** to return to the beginning of the document.

Shrink to Fit

The current document runs to five or six pages. Using the **Shrink to Fit** option reduces the document to fit on one or two pages less. You will see this better if you switch to the Print Preview view.

- Open the **File** menu and choose **Print Preview,** or click the **Print Preview** button.

Currently, there may be only one or two pages displayed. You need to be able to see all the pages at once.

● Click the **Multiple Pages** button.

A small box is opened beneath the button and you can choose how many pages you want to view.

● Click the third square in the second row to give **2 x 3 pages** - if you hold down the mouse button on that square, the text 2 x 3 Pages will appear at the bottom of the box.

All the pages are now shown.

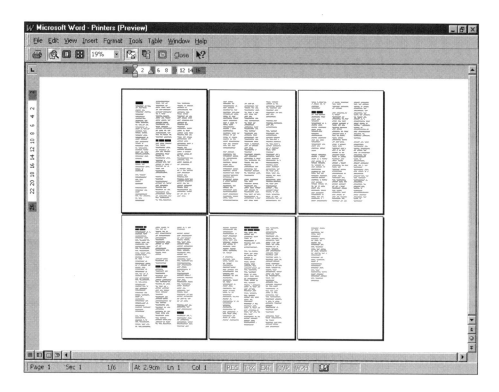

┌───┐
│ ✎ *The exact number of pages you see will depend on the* │
│   *printer you are using.* │
└───┘

● Click the **Shrink to Fit** button.

The document is reduced by one or two pages. You can undo the changes in the normal manner.

- Open the **Edit** menu and choose **Undo Shrink to Fit,** or press **Ctrl+Z.**

Using the Columns dialog box

The Columns dialog box, apart from letting you change the number of columns, lets you set up the width of individual columns and the space between each column.

- Still in the Print Preview view, open the **Format** menu and choose **Columns.**

The Columns dialog box is displayed.

Pre-set column
options

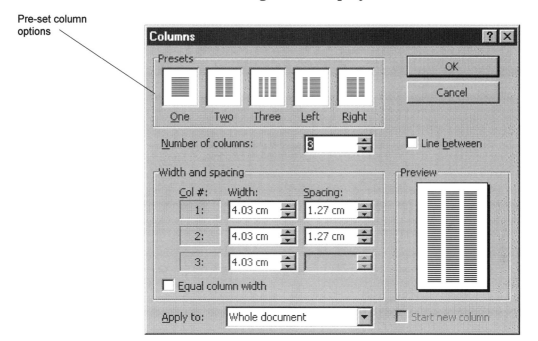

First of all, change to two columns with the left-hand column narrower than the right. To do this you should use the **Left** option in the <u>Presets</u> group of options.

- In the <u>Presets</u> group of options, choose **Left.**

- Click **OK.**

The document is updated, with each page now having two columns.

Adding vertical lines

You can add a vertical line that separates the two columns.

● Open the **Format** menu and choose **Columns**.

The Columns dialog box is displayed again.

● Click the **Line between** option so that it is ticked.

● Click **OK**.

The columns are now separated by a vertical line.

Justifying the columns

Newspaper columns are usually justified. You can justify all the columns in two easy steps, as follows:

● Press **Ctrl+A** to select all the text – on some systems you may not see the selection highlight, but the text is selected.

● Press **Ctrl+J,** to justify the selected text.

● If necessary, click anywhere on a page to remove the selection highlight.

Adjusting the column widths and spacing

You will now adjust the width of column 1 to 5 cm (2") and the spacing to 2.5 cm (1"):

● Open the **Format** menu and choose **Columns**.

The Columns dialog box is displayed again.

● Select the current entry in the Col # 1 Width box, and type:

   5   (or **2** if you are using inches)

● Press the **Tab** key to move to the Spacing box.

The width of column 2 is automatically adjusted to retain the overall width. Now make the gap between the two columns wider. The entry in the Spacing box for column 1 should already have a selection highlight.

● In the Col # 1 Spacing box, type:

2.5   (or **1** if you are using inches)

● Press the **Tab** key to move to the next Width box.

● Click **OK** to apply the changes.

The ruler

Column widths and spacings can be changed using the ruler.

● If necessary, open the **View** menu and choose **Ruler** to display the ruler.

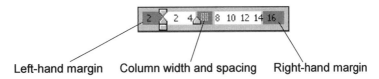

Left-hand margin   Column width and spacing   Right-hand margin

The various parts of the ruler can be used to drag the margins in and out, change the column widths and column spacings. It is probably easier to return to the Page Layout view to do this.

● Click the **Close** button in the Print Preview toolbar.

● Try dragging the various parts of the ruler and see the effect it has on the document – note that the middle button on the ruler has a left edge, centre and right edge, which control different parts of the columns and spacing. If the ruler disappears after an operation, just click the text and it will appear again.

Different columns in the same document

It is easy to have a different number of columns in the same document. You will now apply a single column to selected text.

- Press **Ctrl+Home** to move to the beginning of the document.

- Open the **Zoom** list box and choose **50%**.

- Select the first title, Printers, and all of the first paragraph.

- Click the **Columns** button, and choose the first column.

- Click anywhere on the text to remove the selection highlight.

Only the selected text is changed to have one column. Word automatically creates a clearly marked 'section' for the selected text. This can be seen by switching to the Normal view, then clicking the **Show/Hide ¶** button.

- Open the **View** menu and choose **Normal,** or click the **Normal View** button.

The words Section Break (Continuous) are displayed after the first paragraph. You can now switch back to the Page Layout view.

- Open the **View** menu and choose **Page Layout,** or click the **Page Layout View** button.

The next step is to centre the heading.

- Select the title Printers only.

- Click the **Center** button, or press **Ctrl+E**.

- Click anywhere on the text to remove the selection highlight.

- Open the **Zoom** list box again and choose **100%**.

Next, you will change the last heading and its text to one column.

- Locate the last heading in the document, <u>Printer standards and control codes</u>, and position the insertion point just before the <u>P</u>.

- Open the **Format** menu and choose **Columns**.

The Columns dialog box is displayed. Notice that at the bottom there is an **Apply to** option.

- Open the <u>Apply to</u> list box and choose **This point forward**.

Any changes you make will now only apply from the current position in the text, forwards to the end of the document (or end of the section if the document already has several sections).

- In the <u>Presets</u> group of options, choose **One**.

- Click **OK**.

The last heading and its related text are now in one column only. You can use Print Preview to check the final result.

- Open the **File** menu and choose **Print Preview**, or click the **Print Preview** button.

You should see all the pages at once, with the different numbers of columns.

- When you are ready, click **Close** to close the Print Preview view.

Ending the session

You have now completed the tutorial in this chapter. There is an additional exercise that you may wish to do before moving on to the next chapter or exiting Word. First, you should close the current document.

- Open the **File** menu and choose **Close** – choose **No** to avoid saving the changes.

- If you are not continuing directly with the extra exercise or the next chapter and want to stop now, open the **File** menu and choose **Exit** to exit Word.

Exercise 5a

In this exercise you will practise the column skills you have just learned.

- Open the **Worry** document from your exercise diskette.

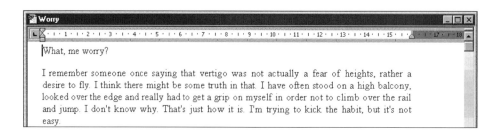

- Before making any changes, save the document on your exercise diskette with the new filename **a:Ex05a**.

Now change the document to four columns.

- Click the **Columns** button.

- Click the fourth column.

The four columns will not be visible unless you are in Page Layout view.

- If necessary, click the **Page Layout View** button.

Now change the heading to one column, centre it and change its formatting.

- Select the heading What, me worry?

- Click the **Columns** button.

- Click the first column.

The heading is now in one column.

- Click the **Center** button.

- Change the format of the heading to **bold** and **underlined** with a font size of **14pt**(or similar).

Now change the rest of the document to two columns of equal width, with a line between.

- Move the insertion point to the start of the first paragraph in the document.

- Open the **Format** menu and choose **Columns**.

- In the Presets group of options, choose **Two**.

- Click the **Line between** option so that it is ticked.

- Check that the **Equal column width** option is ticked.

- Click **OK** to return to the document.

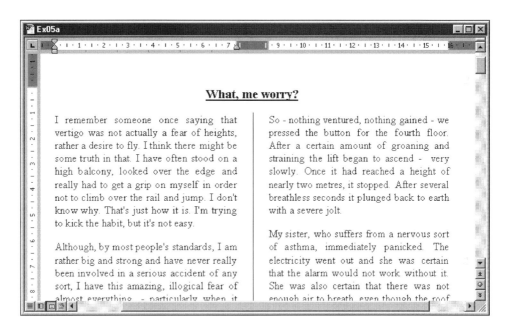

The best way to view the document in its entirety is to use Print Preview.

- Click the **Print Preview** button.

The document probably extends to three pages. Try shrinking it to two pages.

- Click the **Shrink to Fit** button.

The document is reduced by one page.

- Save the document.

- Print the document if you wish.

- When you are ready, close the Print Preview view - click the **Close** button in the Print Preview toolbar.

- Close the document (**File, Close**).

Summary ~ Newspaper Columns

Setting the number of columns on a page

To change the number of columns in a document:

    ✎   Click the **Columns** button

    ✎   Click the required number of columns in the box displayed

More complicated options can be chosen in the Columns dialog box. This is displayed by opening the **Format** menu and choosing **Columns**.

Shrink to Fit

To shrink a document to fit fewer pages:

    ✎   View the document in Print Preview by clicking the **Print Preview** button

    ✎   Click the **Shrink to Fit** button in the Print Preview toolbar

Adding vertical lines between columns

To add vertical lines that separate columns:

    ✎   Open the **Format** menu and choose **Columns**

    ✎   Click the **Line between** option so that it is ticked

Adjusting the width of columns and column spacings

Column widths and spacings can be set in the Columns dialog box. A number of pre-set formats are available, including right and left columns with different widths. The column widths and spacings can also be adjusted using the settings on the ruler.

Different columns in the same document

To have a different number of columns in the same document, either:

    ↳   Select the paragraphs and apply the required number of columns using the **Columns** button

    ↳   Position the insertion point at the start of the section to be changed, then in the Columns dialog box, open the <u>Apply to</u> list box and choose from **This section**, or from **This point forward**

Notes

Use this page to make notes of your own.

Page #   Notes

_____   _____

_____   _____

_____   _____

_____   _____

_____   _____

_____   _____

_____   _____

_____   _____

_____   _____

_____   _____

_____   _____

_____   _____

_____   _____

_____   _____

_____   _____

_____   _____

Chapter 6 ~ Pictures & Text Boxes

Pictures can be inserted into a document at the insertion point. Word also allows you to create text boxes, which can be used for text or other objects. Pictures and text boxes are treated as independent objects that can be moved anywhere in the document.

In this chapter you will learn about:

- ✎ Inserting a picture
- ✎ Scaling a picture
- ✎ Wrapping text around a picture
- ✎ Creating a text box
- ✎ Moving and re-sizing a text box
- ✎ Adding a text box to existing text
- ✎ Wrapping text around a text box

To get started

- If necessary, start your Word program.
- If the Office Assistant is displayed at any time throughout this chapter, you should read what it has to say and then close it – click the **Close** button in the Office Assistant window.
- Open the **Dot Matrix Printers** document from your exercise diskette.

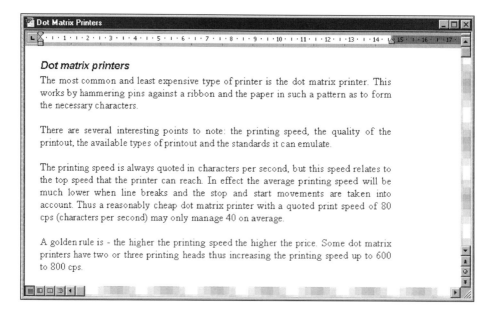

Inserting a picture

You can insert a picture into a document at the insertion point. The picture is then treated as a single character. To do this, you use the **Insert**, **Picture** menu option. Word allows you to insert pictures in different formats from a variety of software packages. These include:

- Windows bitmaps (*.**bmp**)

- Windows metafiles (*.**wmf**)

- Paintbrush (*.**pcx**)

- Tagged Image File Format (*.**tif**)

In this section you will insert the **Matrix** picture supplied on your exercise diskette, into the current document.

The first step is to position the insertion point, as this determines where the picture will be inserted.

- Move the insertion point to the empty line between the first and second paragraphs.

- Open the **Insert** menu and choose **Picture**, then choose **From File**.

The Insert Picture dialog box is displayed.

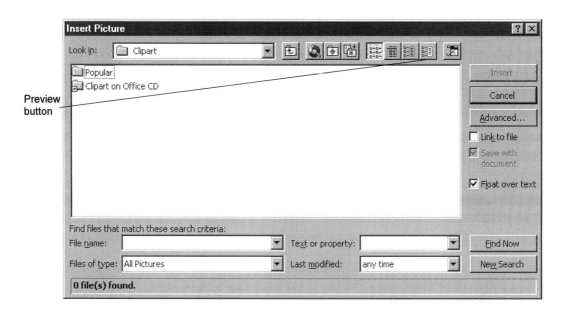

Preview
button

- Open the <u>Files of type</u> list box.

If you scroll the <u>Files of type</u> list, you will see the types of picture files that Word can insert. There is also a useful **All Pictures** option.

- Make sure **All Pictures** is chosen.

- Make sure your exercise diskette is in drive A.

- Open the <u>Look in</u> list box and choose 3½ **Floppy (A:)**.

The available graphics files on the diskette are now listed.

- If necessary, click the **Preview** button in the toolbar.

- In the list of files, choose **Matrix**.

The picture is now shown in the preview box.

- Click **Insert**.

The picture is inserted into the document at the insertion point. It is rather large!

Scaling a picture

A picture can be scaled down or up. It can also be cropped, i.e., have part of it cut away.

- Click anywhere on the picture to select it
  - small squares called *sizing handles* will
  appear around the picture.

- Open the **Format** menu and choose **Picture,** or
  right-click the picture and choose **Format
  Picture.**

The Format Picture dialog box is displayed.

- Click the **Size** tab to show those options.

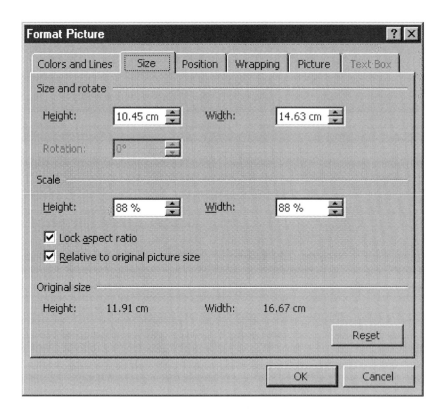

The current <u>Scale</u> values show that the picture is scaled to
88%.

- Change the <u>Scale Height</u> value to **40%.**

- Change the <u>Scale Width</u> value to **40%** – it
  may have automatically changed to 40% when
  you moved out of the <u>Height</u> value box.

♪ *Remember!*
You can use the **Tab** *key to move between the boxes.*

If you choose different scaling values for the width and height, the picture is stretched and does not retain its proportions.

● Click **OK**.

The picture has now been reduced accordingly. You can now move the picture to the centre of the page.

● With the picture still selected, point to the centre of the picture and drag it to the right until it is positioned centrally on the page.

Finally, you can create a little more space above and below the picture by inserting empty lines.

● Move the insertion point to the very end of the first paragraph.

● Press **Enter**.

● Move the insertion point to the very beginning of the second paragraph.

● Press **Enter**.

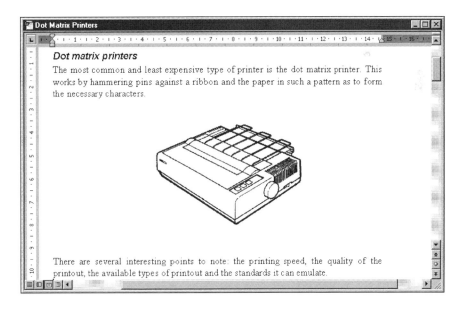

Deleting a picture

Now try deleting the picture.

● Click the picture to select it.

- Press the **Delete** key.

The picture is deleted. You can of course use Undo if you change your mind.

- Open the **Edit** menu and choose **Undo Clear**, or click the **Undo** button, or just press **Ctrl+Z**.

The picture is reinstated.

- Click anywhere on the text to de-select the picture.

Wrapping text

Having inserted a picture, you can drag it around your document and the text will move around the picture.

- Select the picture, then drag it around the document just to see how it is independent of the rest of the document.

You can control how the text moves in relation to the picture by using the **Wrapping** options in the Format Picture dialog box.

- Open the **Format** menu and choose **Picture**, or right-click the picture and choose **Format Picture**.

The Format Picture dialog box is displayed.

- Click the **Wrapping** tab to show those options.

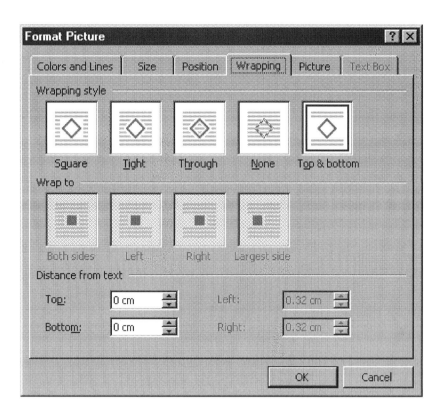

The <u>Wrapping style</u> options allow you to specify where you would like text placed around your picture. In this case you want the text to wrap all of the way around the outside of the picture.

● In the <u>Wrapping style</u> options, choose **Tight**.

● In the <u>Wrap to</u> options, make sure that the **Both sides** option is chosen.

● Click **OK**.

The text moves up around the picture.

● Move the picture around a little and see how the text adjusts itself to wrap around the picture.

Now change the wrapping so that text will only appear above and below the picture.

● Open the **Format** menu and choose **Picture**, or right-click the picture and choose **Format Picture**.

The Format Picture dialog box is displayed again.

- If necessary, click the **Wrapping** tab.

- In the Wrapping style options, choose **Top &
  bottom**.

- Click **OK**.

Finally, move the picture back to its original position
between the first and second paragraphs.

- Drag the picture so that it appears between
  the first and second paragraphs again.

- Click anywhere on the text to de-select the
  picture.

Text boxes

Text boxes are useful because they act like independent
objects in the document. You can move, re-size and format
text boxes without any regard for the text in the rest of the
document. A text box can contain text, or other objects
such as an Excel spreadsheet.

Creating a text box

To create a text box, you choose the **Text Box** option in
the **Insert** menu and simply drag out a text box of the
desired size in roughly the place you want it. You can
move and re-size a text box at any time, so you don't have
to worry about getting it exactly right first time.

To work with text boxes you must be in the Page Layout
view.

- If necessary, open the **View** menu and choose
  Page Layout, or click the **Page Layout View**
  button.

You can now create a text box.

- Open the **Insert** menu and choose **Text Box**.

Nothing happens immediately, but when you position the
mouse pointer over the document area it changes to a
hairline cross, ready for you to drag out a text box.

- Move the mouse pointer to the left of the picture and drag out a small text box across the document - check the following picture for guidance.

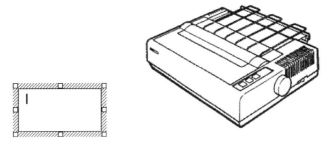

You should now have an empty text box with a diagonally-striped border around it. There will be a flashing insertion point inside the text box ready for you to type something.

- Type:

A matrix printer

Text inside a text box can be formatted in the usual manner.

- Click the **Center** button, or press **Ctrl+E**.

- Select the text inside the text box.

- Open the **Font Size** list box and choose **18**.

- Click the **Bold** button, or press **Ctrl+B**.

- Click anywhere outside the text box to de-activate it.

The insertion point is no longer available and the diagonally-striped border around the text box has disappeared. The text box is no longer active. Do not worry if the text box is positioned in the next paragraph, or if part of the text is not visible; you can easily move and re-size it.

Moving and re-sizing a text box

A text box can be re-sized and moved, or dragged, to any position on a page. To do either of these things, you must first select the text box so that the *sizing handles* are visible.

- Click anywhere on the text box so that the sizing handles appear.

Sizing handle ——————

The *sizing handles* are the eight small squares positioned around the edge of the text box. They are used for re-sizing the text box. The rest of the text box border can be used to move the text box.

First, you will resize the text box. As you move the mouse pointer over a sizing handle, the pointer changes to a small double-headed arrow showing which way the text box can be re-sized using that handle.

- Position the mouse pointer over the bottom centre frame handle.

The mouse pointer changes to a double-headed arrow.

- Click and drag the handle down slightly, so that you can read all the text in the box.

A matrix printer

Now try moving the text box.

- Position the mouse pointer somewhere on the border of the text box, but not on one of the sizing handles.

The mouse pointer changes to a left-pointing arrow with crossed double-headed arrows.

- Drag the text box upwards so that it lines up with the middle of the picture.

Formatting a text box

You will now format the text box so that it does not have a border.

- Make sure the text box is selected.

- Open the **Format** menu and choose **Text Box,** or right-click the frame around the text box and choose **Format Text Box.**

The Format Text Box dialog box is displayed. You need to use the **Colors and Lines** options.

- If necessary, click the **Colors and Lines** tab to show those options.

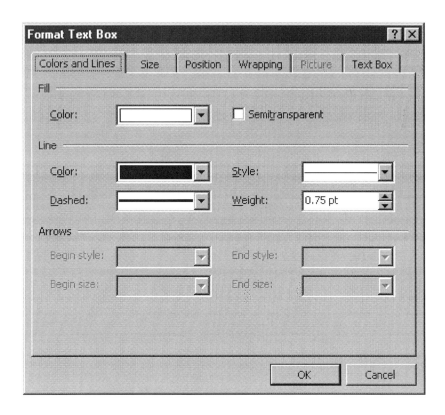

- In the <u>Line</u> options, open the <u>Color</u> list box and choose **No Line.**

- Click **OK**.

- Click anywhere on the document to de-select the text box.

The text box now has no border.

Deleting a text box

To delete any text box, select it so that the *sizing handles* and the *fuzzy frame* appear, and then press the **Delete** key.

- Select the text box - when selected, its sizing handles are visible and it is surrounded by a fuzzy frame.

- Press the **Delete** key.

The text box is deleted, together with the text that was in it.

Adding a text box to existing text

If you already have text, but want to put it in a text box, you can select the text and then choose the **Insert**, **Text Box** menu option. However, don't mix up two different concepts.

     ☟   If you want to give a paragraph a border, you don't have to put it in a text box - just use the Borders options

     ☟   If you want to create an independent section of text that you can move around in the document, put it in a text box

In this example, you will select an existing paragraph and put it in a text box, just to see how it works.

- Scroll the document downwards until you find the paragraph Colour dot matrix printers are now available.

- Select the whole paragraph.

- Open the **Insert** menu and choose **Text Box**.

A text box is created with the selected text inside.

- Drag the new text box around the document just to see that it is now independent of the rest of the text.

Text flow around a text box

How the text flows around a text box will considerably affect the look of your document. As for pictures, you can change the way text appears around the outside of a text box.

- Make sure that the new text box you have just created is selected.

The text will probably flow around the current text box. You can change this in the Format Text Box dialog box.

- Open the **Format** menu and choose **Text Box,** or right-click the frame surrounding the text box and choose **Format Text box** in the shortcut menu.

The Format Text Box dialog box is displayed. You need to display the **Wrapping** options.

- If necessary, click the **Wrapping** tab to display those options.

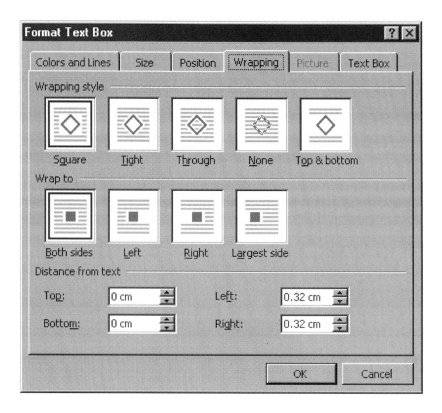

- In the Wrapping style options, choose
  Square.

- In the Wrap to options, choose **Largest
  side**.

You can govern the distance between the text box and the
surrounding text by using the Distance from text options.

- In the Distance from text options, change
  the value in the Top box to **1 cm** (or **0.5"**
  if you are using inches).

- Click **OK**.

- Move the text box around and notice the
  effect on the surrounding text.

- When you are ready, click outside of the
  text box to remove the selection frame.

Ending the session

You have now completed the tutorial in this chapter. There is an additional exercise that you may wish to do before moving on to the next chapter or exiting Word. First, you should close the current document.

● Open the **File** menu and choose **Close** - choose **No** to avoid saving the changes.

● If you are not continuing directly with the extra exercise or the next chapter and want to stop now, open the **File** menu and choose **Exit** to exit Word.

Exercise 6a

In this exercise you will insert a picture in a document, and move it into the text. You will then create a text box and insert some text.

● Open the **Orville Wright** document from your exercise diskette.

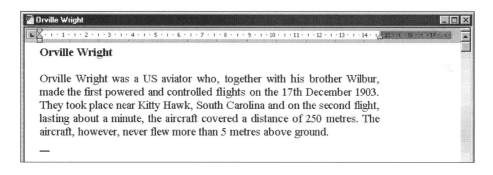

● Press **Enter** twice to create a space at the top of the document.

● Move the insertion point to the top of the document - **Ctrl+Home.**

● Open the **Insert** menu and choose **Picture,** and then choose **From File.**

● In the Insert Picture dialog box, choose the file **Flyace.wmf** - it is on your exercise diskette.

The picture is inserted at the top of the document. Now, reduce the size of the picture and move it into the body of the text.

- Click the picture to select it.

- Open the **Format** menu and choose **Picture**, then click the **Size** tab.

- In the Scale options, change the Width and Height to **50%**.

- Click **OK**.

The picture is reduced in size. Now move it into the text.

- Drag the picture into the text so that it is at the start of the paragraph.

You can now experiment with the text wrapping.

- Right-click the picture and choose **Format Picture** in the shortcut menu.

- Click the **Wrapping** tab to show those options.

- In the Wrapping style options, choose **Tight**.

- Click **OK**.

Note how the text has moved around the picture. Finally, put a border around the picture and type a heading within the picture.

- Right-click the picture and choose **Format Picture** in the shortcut menu.

- Click the **Colors and Lines** tab.

- In the Line options, open the Color list box and choose a **blue** colour.

- Click **OK**.

- Click anywhere on the text to remove the selection highlight.

Now you can insert a text box on the banner.

- Open the **Insert** menu and choose **Text Box**.

- Drag out a box within the banner and type:

   Flying Ace

- Select the text and change its formatting to **Bold** with a font size of **12pts.**

Finally, remove the border around the text frame.

- Right-click the frame surrounding the text box and choose **Format Text Box.**

- Click the **Colors and Lines** tab.

- In the Line options, open the Color list box and choose **No Line.**

- Click **OK.**

- Click anywhere on the document to remove the selection highlight.

Your document should now resemble the next picture.

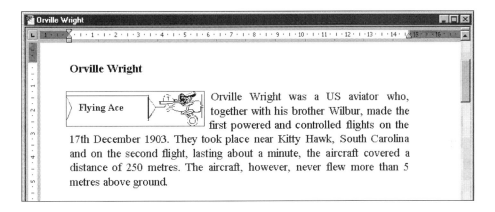

You can now save and close the document. You may print it if you wish.

- Save the document on your exercise diskette, with the new filename **a:Ex06a.**

- Print the document if you wish, or just use Print Preview to view it.

- Close the document (**File, Close**).

Summary ~ Pictures & Text Boxes

Inserting a picture

To insert a picture in a document:

- ✎   Position the insertion point where you want the picture to be

- ✎   Open the **Insert** menu and choose **Picture**, and then choose **From File**

- ✎   Use the Insert Picture dialog box to find the file you require

Scaling a picture

To scale a picture:

- ✎   Select the picture

- ✎   Open the **Format** menu and choose **Picture**

- ✎   Click the **Size** tab, then change the <u>Width</u> and <u>Height</u> scaling as appropriate

Wrapping text around a picture

Having inserted a picture, you can move it freely around your document. How the text appears around the picture is governed by the **Wrapping** options in the Format Picture dialog box.

- ✎   Select the picture

- ✎   Open the **Format** menu and choose **Picture**, or right-click the text box and choose **Format Picture**

- ✎   Click the **Wrapping** tab to show those options

- ✎   Using the <u>Wrapping style</u> options, choose how you would like the text wrapped around the outside of your object

Creating a text box

To create a text box:

- ✍ Open the **Insert** menu and choose **Text Box**
- ✍ Drag out a text box using the mouse
- ✍ Type your required text into the text box

The text can be formatted in any of the usual ways.

Moving and re-sizing a text box

To move or re-size a text box or picture object, the sizing handles must be visible. To display these:

- ✍ Click the text box once to select it - the sizing handles will appear

To move a text box, position the mouse over the diagonally-striped border and drag the text box to where you require it.

To re-size a text box, drag one of the sizing handles in or out as appropriate.

Formatting text boxes

Borders and shading effects can be added to text boxes as follows:

- ✍ Select the text box
- ✍ Open the **Format** menu and choose **Text Box**, or right-click the text box and choose **Format Text Box**
- ✍ Click the **Colors and Lines** tab and make your choices for the lines and colours outside and within the box

Adding a text box to existing text

To add a text box to existing text:

- ✍ Select the text
- ✍ Open the **Insert** menu and choose **Text Box**

The text can then be moved around independently.

Wrapping text around a text box

The text wrapping attribute is set in the Format Text Box dialog box.

        ꝃ   Select the text box

        ꝃ   Open the **Format** menu and choose **Text Box**, or right-click the text box and choose **Format Text Box**

        ꝃ   Click the **Wrapping** tab to show those options

        ꝃ   Using the <u>Wrapping style</u> options, choose how you would like the text wrapped around the outside of your object

Notes

Use this page to make notes of your own.

Page #   Notes

_____   _____

_____   _____

_____   _____

_____   _____

_____   _____

_____   _____

_____   _____

_____   _____

_____   _____

_____   _____

_____   _____

_____   _____

_____   _____

_____   _____

Notes

Use this page to make notes of your own.

Page #   Notes

_____   _____

_____   _____

_____   _____

_____   _____

_____   _____

_____   _____

_____   _____

_____   _____

_____   _____

_____   _____

_____   _____

_____   _____

_____   _____

_____   _____

_____   _____

Chapter 7 ~ Desktop Publishing

In the previous three chapters you have learnt about columns, borders, pictures and text boxes. Desktop publishing is the bringing together of text and pictures to create a finished article. In this chapter you will combine text with a picture, using columns, text boxes and shading, to create a simple one page article.

In this chapter you will re-use the following skills:

ᕳ   Setting different numbers of columns on one page

ᕳ   Creating and formatting a text box

ᕳ   Adding a picture

ᕳ   Applying borders and shading features

It is assumed that:

ᕳ   You know the basics about columns, borders, shading, pictures and text boxes as covered in the previous chapters

To get started

●   If necessary, start your Word program.

●   If the Office Assistant is displayed at any time throughout this chapter, you should read what it has to say and then close it – click the **Close** button in the Office Assistant window.

●   Open the **Home Security** document from your exercise diskette.

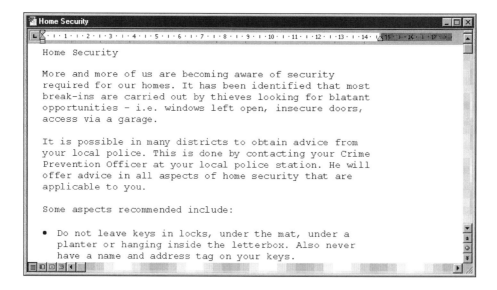

```
Home Security                                               _ □ ×
L        1   2   3   4   5   6   7   8   9   10   11   12   13   14   15   16   17

Home Security

More and more of us are becoming aware of security
required for our homes. It has been identified that most
break-ins are carried out by thieves looking for blatant
opportunities - i.e. windows left open, insecure doors,
access via a garage.

It is possible in many districts to obtain advice from
your local police. This is done by contacting your Crime
Prevention Officer at your local police station. He will
offer advice in all aspects of home security that are
applicable to you.

Some aspects recommended include:

•  Do not leave keys in locks, under the mat, under a
   planter or hanging inside the letterbox. Also never
   have a name and address tag on your keys.
```

The task

A copy of exactly what you are trying to create is shown on the next page. The main features are:

    ✎   The title and the first three paragraphs are in one column. They are formatted in various ways, with different alignments

    ✎   The rest of the document comprises two equal columns, with a vertical line between

    ✎   A picture is inserted in the centre of the document, with the text flowing around it

    ✎   There is a text box at the foot of the second column

Formatting the text

Start off by selecting a font for the whole document.

●   Press **Ctrl+A** to select the whole document.

●   Open the **Font** list box and choose **Times New Roman** (or other font if you can't find this one).

The font for the whole text is changed.

Formatting the title

The title needs to be formatted as shown.

- Format the title, <u>Home Security</u>, as **bold, centred** and **36pt**.

- Display the Tables and Borders toolbar.

- Put a **3pt** border around the title and apply **25%** shading.

- Hide the Tables and Borders toolbar.

Home Security

More and more of us are becoming aware of security required for our homes. It has been identified that most break-ins are carried out by thieves looking for blatant opportunities - windows left open, insecure doors, access via a garage.

It is possible in many districts to obtain advice from your local police. This is done by contacting your Crime Prevention Officer at your local police station. He will offer advice in all aspects of home security that are applicable to you.

Some aspects recommended include:

- Do not leave keys in locks, under the mat, under a planter or hanging inside the letterbox. Also never have a name and address tag on your keys.

- Never leave windows open should you go out.

- Fit locks to windows near drainpipes, trees, flat roofs or anywhere else that is easily accessible.

- Garages are often used as a point of entry if there is an internal door to the house. Ensure that the Garage is always securely locked and fit a lock to any door linking to the house.

- Be sure to cancel milk and newspapers should you be going away.

- Arrange for a neighbour to look after the property, removing any leaflets or free newspapers which may be protruding from the letterbox.

- Keep ladders locked away.

- Hedges, shrubs and trees should not be permitted to grow to shield the house from view. A thief will take advantage of not being able to be viewed by neighbours.

- Obtain an ultra-violet marking pen to print your house number and postcode onto any valuables. This assists the police if the items are found at a later date.

- Ensure that sheds are securely locked. Tools stored in them may be used to assist with a break-in.

Remember!
Lock it or Lose it!

Formatting the first three paragraphs

The first three paragraphs need formatting with different font sizes and alignments.

- Format the first paragraph as **bold, 14pt** and **centred.**

- Format the second paragraph as **bold, 12pt** and **centred.**

- Format the third paragraph as **bold, 14pt** and **left-aligned.**

The first paragraph would look better if the examples of blatant opportunities were on a separate line. You will put in a manual line break and at the same time delete the text i.e..

- Select the characters i.e. and press **Shift+Enter.**

The top of your document should now resemble the following picture.

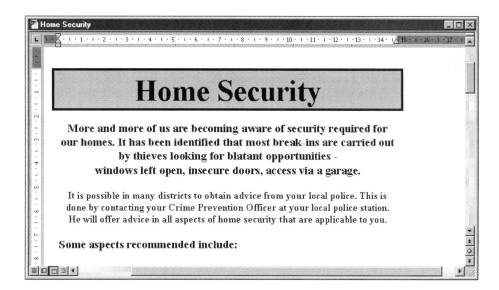

Creating the columns

From the beginning of the fourth paragraph onwards, the document should be divided into two columns. You can either use the Columns dialog box, or select the text first and then use the **Columns** button. In this example you will use the dialog box because this allows you to choose the vertical line at the same time.

- Move the insertion point to the very beginning of the fourth paragraph – immediately before the words Do not.

- Open the **Format** menu and choose **Columns**.

The Columns dialog box is displayed.

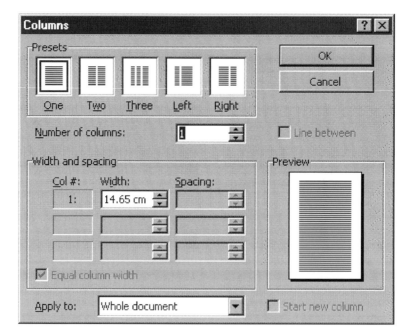

First, make sure you change the number of columns from the insertion point forwards, and not for the whole document.

- Open the Apply to list box and choose **This point forward**.

- In the Presets group of options, choose **Two**.

- If necessary, click the **Line between** option so that it is ticked.

- Click **OK**.

The columns are created. If you are in the Normal view, you won't see the columns side-by-side, but you will see a <u>Section Break</u> marker.

- If necessary, open the **View** menu and choose **Page Layout**, or click the **Page Layout View** button.

The columns are now visible side-by-side. Try zooming out to see more of the document at once:

- Open the **Zoom** list box and choose **50%**.

The document is taking shape!

Inserting a picture

It's now time to insert a picture. You will be using the picture, **Houses.wmf**, which can be found on your exercise diskette.

- Open the **Insert** menu and choose **Picture**, then choose **From File**.

The Insert Picture dialog box is displayed.

- From your exercise diskette, choose the file **Houses**.

The picture is inserted into the document at your current insertion point - it may have been inserted in a different place to the example shown in the following picture.

Scaling the picture

Next, you will change the scaling of the picture.

- With the picture selected, open the **Format** menu and choose **Picture**.

The Format Picture dialog box is displayed.

- Click the **Size** tab.

- In the <u>Scale</u> options, change the <u>Height</u> and the <u>Width</u> to **180%**.

- Click **OK**.

- Re-position the picture so that it is in the middle of the document - just drag it to the centre of the document.

Wrapping the text around the picture

You may have found that the text does not wrap around the picture. To rectify this, you need to use the **Wrapping** options in the Format Picture dialog box.

- With the picture still selected, open the **Format** menu and choose **Picture**.

The Format Picture dialog box is displayed again.

- Click the **Wrapping** tab to show those options.

- In the <u>Wrapping style</u> options, choose **Square**.

- In the <u>Wrap to</u> options, make sure that **Both sides** is chosen.

- Click **OK**.

- Click anywhere on the text to de-select the picture.

Creating the text box

The last feature you need to create is the text box at the bottom of the second column.

- Keep the 50% view and, if necessary, scroll down the display so that you can see the bottom of the page.

- Open the **Insert** menu and choose **Text Box.**

- Drag out a text box covering the bottom right-hand corner of the document, keeping it roughly in line with the columns.

- In the text box, type:

  Remember!
  Lock it or Lose it!

- Format the text as **bold, 24pt** and **centred.**

- Resize the text box so that you can read the text.

The text box should now look like this:

> **Remember!**
> **Lock it or Lose it!**

Formatting the text box

Finally, format the frame surrounding the text box.

- Open the **Format** menu and choose **Text Box.**

The Format Text Box dialog box is displayed.

- Click the **Colors and Lines** tab.

- In the Line options, change the line Weight to **3pt.**

- Click **OK.**

Finishing off

All that is left to do now is to tidy up.

- On your own, make any small adjustments to improve the look of the final document.

- When you are ready, zoom the display back to 100%.

- If you want to, save your document on your exercise diskette with the name **a:My Security**.

- When you are ready, print the document.

Ending the session

You have now completed the tutorial in this chapter. There is an additional exercise that you may wish to do before moving on to the next chapter or exiting Word. First, you should close the current document.

- Open the **File** menu and choose **Close**.

- If you are not continuing directly with the extra exercise or the next chapter and want to stop now, open the **File** menu and choose **Exit** to exit Word.

Exercise 7a

- Use the files **Costa del Fortune** and **Spain** on your exercise diskette to create the document shown on the next page.

- When you have finished, save the document as **a:Ex07a** and then print it.

The Costa del Fortune

What with runaway criminals, alleged drug money, tax exiles and pure drunken tourism, Spain's Costa del Sol has been the subject of much speculation of late.

La Costa seems to have become the southern European playground of the newly rich, the wish-I-was-newly-rich, and those looking for sunstroke in a comfortable carpet slippers and fish and chips environment. You know the syndrome - "It's great in Spain, just like 'ome only 'otter".

Watney's Red Barrel and tea like mother used to make may well flow in the bars and cafés of Fuengirola, Los Boliches, Torremolinos and Benalmadena, but you shouldn't go away with the impression that it is only the British that have transformed this one-time sleepy fishing coast into a Blackpool on wheels.

The Germans, Scandinavians, Dutch, and even the Americans, (here read Euro-fizz, Budweiser etc.) all have their own ghettos and spheres of influence. All recount their own version of why Spain has gone to the dogs and all are equally oblivious of the culture, history and tradition that laps at their feet.

Marbella, Puerto Banus and Soto Grande have for some time been the playground of Europe's 2nd Division of beautiful people, and the Costa del Sol has long been the goal of northern European pensioners trying to eke out their meagre fixed incomes and live in a style to which they would like to become accustomed.

However, whilst Europe and the Western World have been going through a period of enlightenment, greater unity and reduction of tension, the void between Spain and its foreign residents seems to be widening.

Spain's entry into the European Community has obviously left its mark. The event may have been applauded by those foreign residents who assumed that life would become even easier once the Spaniards "come up to our standard" - "my dear, they really are learning fast"! However, it is a painful and pathetic fact that the majority of foreign residents have failed, even after many years residence, to learn the language. Even more tragic is the fact that they have failed - and continue to fail - to contribute anything of value to Spain, its environment or its development. The modern Spaniard is not a fool, he can read the writing on the gin bottle as well as the next man - and quite justifiably, he resents what he sees!

Next week: Mirabella reports from Alassio on the Italian Riviera!

Notes

Use this page to make notes of your own.

Page #   Notes

_____   _____

_____   _____

_____   _____

_____   _____

_____   _____

_____   _____

_____   _____

_____   _____

_____   _____

_____   _____

_____   _____

_____   _____

_____   _____

_____   _____

_____   _____

_____   _____

Chapter 8 ~ Report Writing

In your everyday work, you may often want to produce reports, etc. In this chapter you will create a set of minutes, using some of the features Word provides to help you. You will also create a table of contents.

In this chapter you will learn about:

- ✎ Heading styles and numbering
- ✎ Indenting paragraphs
- ✎ Using the Outline view
- ✎ Moving sections up and down
- ✎ Promoting and demoting sections
- ✎ Inserting a table of contents

Getting started

- If necessary, start your Word program.

- If the Office Assistant is displayed at any time throughout this chapter, you should read what it has to say and then close it – click the **Close** button in the Office Assistant window.

- Open the **Minutes** document from your exercise diskette.

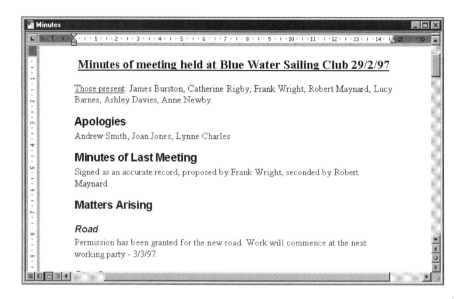

Using styles

In your everyday work, you may sometimes need to write reports with a hierarchy of sub-sections and numbered headings. You will see that the **Minutes** document uses different heading styles. These heading styles are provided by the Normal template in Word. If you use these styles when you write a document, it is easy to number sections and sub-sections. You can also use the Outline view to display the document down to a specific heading level. You will start by looking at two headings in this document.

●   Position the insertion point in the heading Matters Arising.

Notice that the **Style** box in the left-hand end of the Formatting toolbar reads <u>Heading 1</u>.

●   Position the insertion point in the heading Road.

This time the **Style** box reads <u>Heading 2</u>.

Numbering headings

At present, none of the headings are numbered. The document would look a lot clearer if they were. To do this:

    ✎   Open the **Format** menu and choose **Bullets and Numbering** to display the Bullets and Numbering dialog box

    ✎   Click the **Outline Numbered** tab

    ✎   Choose the numbering style you require and click **OK**

You can try this now. First, you need to make sure that your insertion point is positioned where you want your first number to appear.

- Make sure your insertion point is positioned immediately before the A in the word Apologies - the first Heading 1.

- Open the **Format** menu and choose **Bullets and Numbering**.

The Bullets and Numbering dialog box is displayed.

- Click the **Outline Numbered** tab to show those options.

Here you can choose a style for numbering your report.

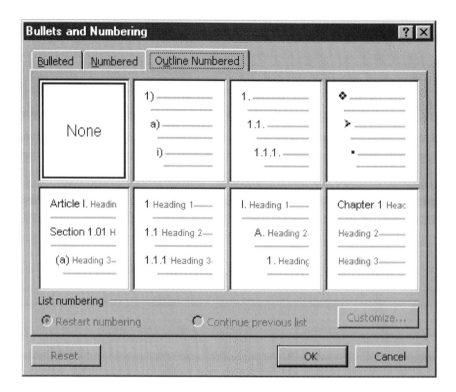

- Choose the second style in the bottom row, i.e.,
  1 Heading 1, 1.1 Heading 2, 1.1.1 Heading 3.

- Click **OK**, or press **Enter**.

The headings are now numbered as shown in the next picture.

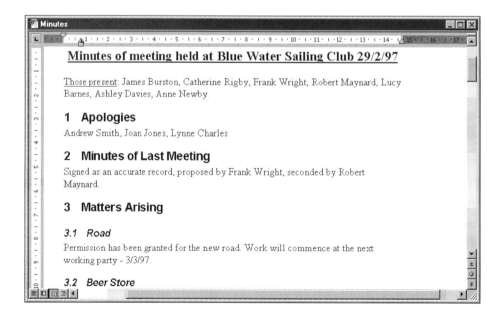

Indenting paragraphs

The next step is to indent the paragraphs to match the indented headings. This is done using the **Increase Indent** button - if you use the **Tab** key, only the first line of the paragraph will be indented.

- Position the insertion point in the paragraph starting Andrew Smith.

- Click the **Increase Indent** button once.

The text is now lined up under the heading title Apologies. Now indent the second paragraph to match the heading Minutes of Last Meeting.

- Position the insertion point in the paragraph starting Signed as an accurate record.

- Click the **Increase Indent** button once.

The paragraphs for the Road and the Beer Store also need to be indented to line up with their respective headings. You can do this now.

- Position the insertion point in the paragraph starting Permission has been granted.

- Click the **Increase Indent** button.

Using the Format Painter

As you may recall, the Format Painter can be used to copy text and paragraph formatting from one section of text to another. This is particularly useful when the formatting involves several features.

- Select the paragraph starting Permission has been granted (triple-click anywhere in the paragraph).

- Click the **Format Painter** button.

- Click once anywhere in the following paragraph, A new cooler.

The format is copied and the second paragraph is aligned correctly.

> **2 Minutes of Last Meeting**
>
> Signed as an accurate record, proposed by Frank Wright, seconded by Robert Maynard.
>
> **3 Matters Arising**
>
> *3.1 Road*
>
> Permission has been granted for the new road. Work will commence at the next working party - 3/3/97.
>
> *3.2 Beer Store*
>
> A new cooler has been purchased.

Adding sub-sections

Sometimes when you are compiling a report, you will realise that some information has been omitted. This is easy to rectify. For example, if you want to add a sub-section to an existing section:

- ✎ Insert a new line

- ✎ Position the insertion point at the start of the line

- ✎ Open the **Style** list box and choose the heading style you require

- ✎ Type your sub-heading

The Commodore's report is incomplete. You will now add two sub-sections to it.

- ● Move the insertion point to the end of the heading Commodore - James Burston.

- ● Press **Enter** to start a new line.

- ● Open the **Style** list box and choose **Heading 3**.

The section number 4.1.1 is inserted into the document, and the insertion point is positioned ready for you to type the sub-heading.

- ● Type:

  World Championships in Dubai

- ● Press **Enter**.

Now add a second sub-heading.

- Open the **Style** list box and choose **Heading 3.**

The section number 4.1.2 is inserted into the document, and the insertion point is positioned ready for you to type the next sub-heading.

- Type:

Work Parties

Adding text

Before you start to enter the text for these sub-sections of the minutes, you need to indent the paragraph.

- Move the insertion point to the end of the heading World Championships in Dubai and press **Enter**.

- Click the **Increase Indent** button three times.

- Type:

  The BWSC team has been training over the winter. The boats have been shipped. The team will fly out on 3/4/97.

Now you will complete the sub-section on Work Parties.

- Move the insertion point to the end of the heading Work Parties.

- Press **Enter**.

- Use the **Increase Indent** button to indent the paragraph to match the previous sub-section.

- Type:

  Progressing well though turn-out below last year. All people who did not attend will be asked to help with jetty building later in the summer. AD to compile a list of these people from the database. LB to set up summer work parties.

Inserting a new sub-heading

If you insert a new sub-section within a list of existing sub-sections, Word will renumber the headings to accommodate the insertion. You can try this now. Insert an extra section in the Treasurer's report for the Deposit account balance.

- Position the insertion point just before the heading Subscriptions.

- Press **Enter**.

Word provides you with the heading number 4.3.2 and renumbers the other two headings in this section of the report. You can now type the heading and the text. Word will format the heading with the style Heading 3. However, you will have to indent the associated paragraph correctly.

- In the newly created section, type:

  Deposit account

- Press **Enter**.

- Click the **Increase Indent** button three times.

- Type:

  At 28/2/97: £15,800

The text of the minutes is now complete. However, there are still a few changes to make concerning the order of the sections and the priority of some sub-sections. This is most easily achieved in the Outline view.

Outline view

The Outline view provides a view of your document in which you can choose to view the whole document, or just the headings down to a specific level. This is very useful for providing an overview of a long document. It enables you to move sections around easily and promote or demote headings to a different level. As usual, the best way to learn is by example. You can now look at the Minutes document in the Outline view.

- Move the insertion point to the top of the document (**Ctrl+Home**).

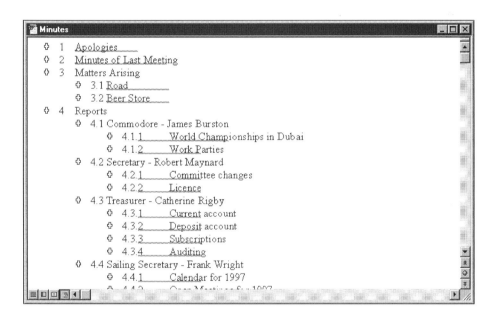

- Open the **View** menu and choose **Outline,** or click the **Outline View** button.

The document is displayed in the Outline view. A toolbar of useful buttons is displayed.

- Move the mouse pointer over the toolbar buttons without clicking them, and read what each one does.

- If necessary, click the **Show All Headings** button so that it is not chosen.

- If necessary, click the **Show Formatting** button so that it is not chosen.

```
Minutes                                              _ □ ×
   ⊕  1   Apologies
   ⊕  2   Minutes of Last Meeting
   ⊕  3   Matters Arising
          ⊕  3.1 Road
          ⊕  3.2 Beer Store
   ⊕  4   Reports
          ⊕  4.1 Commodore - James Burston
                 ⊕  4.1.1      World Championships in Dubai
                 ⊕  4.1.2      Work Parties
          ⊕  4.2 Secretary - Robert Maynard
                 ⊕  4.2.1      Committee changes
                 ⊕  4.2.2      Licence
          ⊕  4.3 Treasurer - Catherine Rigby
                 ⊕  4.3.1      Current account
                 ⊕  4.3.2      Deposit account
                 ⊕  4.3.3      Subscriptions
                 ⊕  4.3.4      Auditing
          ⊕  4.4 Sailing Secretary - Frank Wright
                 ⊕  4.4.1      Calendar for 1997
                 ⊕  4.4.2      Open Meetings for 1997
```

- Scroll the document to examine its contents.

The fuzzy lines displayed under headings show the presence of text.

Displaying different levels

In the Outline view you can choose to display the headings down to specific levels. This is done by clicking the appropriate **Show Heading** button. To display all the document, you have to click the **Show All Headings** button.

- Click the `Show All Headings` button.

The whole document is displayed in the Outline view. Now try out some of the **Show Heading** buttons.

- Click the `Show Heading 2` button.

The document is displayed with all Heading 1 and Heading 2 headings visible. It is interesting to note that the main heading of the document is not displayed. This is because it was formatted separately and was not assigned one of the pre-set styles from the Normal template. Now just display the Heading 1 style headings.

- Click the `Show Heading 1` button.

Expanding

In the Outline view, a ✛ sign is used to indicate that a particular section has sub-sections and body text. The **Expand** button is used to display these. A heading with a □ sign has no sub-sections nor text associated with it. To display all the sub-sections and body text of a particular heading:

- ↳ Select the complete section heading - click the selection bar to the left of the ✛ sign

- ↳ Click the **Expand** button

To reveal the sub-sections one level at a time:

- ↳ Position the insertion point in the section heading

- ↳ Click the **Expand** button once to reveal the next level down

- ↳ Continue clicking the **Expand** button to reveal the other levels in turn

You can try both these methods now. First, expand the section <u>Reports</u> to reveal the next level down.

●   `Click anywhere in the heading `<u>`Reports`</u>`.`

●   `Click the `**`Expand`**` button.`

The section is expanded to show the sub-sections 4.1 to 4.4. Now expand the whole of the sub-section 4.1 to reveal all sub-sections and the body text.

●   `Select the heading for section 4.1,`
      <u>`Commodore - James Burston`</u>` - click the`
      `selection bar to the left of the ⇧ sign to`
      `select the whole heading.`

●   `Click the `**`Expand`**` button.`

The section is expanded to show both sub-sections and the associated body text. You can also choose to display the first line of the text only.

●   `Click the `**`Show First Line Only`**` button.`

The first line of each paragraph is displayed. The ellipsis (three dots) at the end of each line of text indicates that there is more text in this particular paragraph.

●   `Click the `**`Show First Line Only`**` button`
      `again.`

The paragraph is now shown in full again.

Collapsing

There are two rules for collapsing a section - which are similar to those for expanding a section:

   🖏   To collapse the whole section, select the complete section heading - click the selection bar to the left of the ⌐ sign - and then click the **Collapse** button

   🖏   To collapse the section one level at a time, position the insertion point in the section heading, and then click the **Collapse** button once for each level to be collapsed

You will now try this out on section 4.1.2.

●   `Click anywhere in the heading `<u>`Work Parties`</u>`.`

● Click the **Collapse** button.

The sub-section headed <u>Work Parties</u> is collapsed to display its heading only. Now collapse the whole <u>Reports</u> section.

● Select the heading <u>Reports</u> - click to the <u>left</u> of the ⇧ sign in the selection bar to select the whole heading.

● Click the **Collapse** button.

The <u>Reports</u> heading is displayed with no sub-headings and no body text, just like the other section headings in the document.

Moving a section up

In the Outline view, it is easy to move sections around. However, it is important to remember that when you move a section up, it will move above the section that is currently displayed above it. Consequently, if you want to move a Heading 1 section up and keep it at the same level, you should have only the Heading 1 style headings displayed.

To demonstrate how easy it is to move sections around, you can move the <u>Newsletter</u> heading above the <u>Yearbook</u> heading. This will move the text associated with each heading, and renumber the headings as well.

● If necessary, click the **Show Heading 1** button.

● Click anywhere in the heading <u>Newsletter</u>.

● Click the **Move Up** button once.

The <u>Newsletter</u> section is moved up, and both headings are renumbered.

```
┌─────────────────────────────────────────────────────────────────┐
│ ▓ Minutes                                              _ □ ☒      │
├─────────────────────────────────────────────────────────────────┤
│  ⇧  1   Apologies........                                      ▲  │
│  ⇧  2   Minutes of Last Meeting                                │  │
│  ⇧  3   Matters Arising.....                                   │  │
│  ⇧  4   Reports........                                        │  │
│  ⇧  5   [Newsletter]                                           │  │
│  ⇧  6   Yearbook........                                       │  │
│  ▭  7   Any Other Business                                     │  │
│  ⇧  8   Dogs........                                           │  │
│  ⇧  9   Date of Next Meeting                                  │  │
│  ━━                                                           ▼  │
└─────────────────────────────────────────────────────────────────┘
```

If you wish, you can confirm that the text has moved as
well.

- Click the **Show All Headings** button.

- When you are ready, click the **Show All
  Headings** button again.

Moving a section down

When you wish to move a section down, the same rules
apply; you should only display the headings down to the
level of those you wish to move. This time, you want to
move the section about the Secretary's report below that of
the Treasurer. These are Heading 2 style headings.

- Click the **Show Heading 2** button.

- Click anywhere in the heading Secretary –
  Robert Maynard.

- Click the **Move Down** button.

The heading is moved down and both headings are
renumbered.

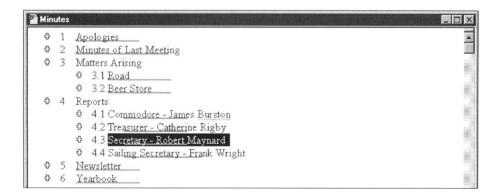

To check that the sub-sections have been renumbered too, you need to display the Heading 3 style headings.

- Click the **Show Heading 3** button.

Displaying formatting

In the Outline view, you can display the formatting of the headings. Just click the **Show Formatting** button. Each level of heading is then easy to distinguish from the rest.

- Click the **Show Formatting** button.

The headings are displayed with their various formats.

✥ **4 Reports**
    ✥ *4.1 Commodore - James Burston*
        ✥ 4.1.1   World Championships in Dubai
        ✥ 4.1.2   Work Parties

Demoting a section

Sometimes when you write a report, you may decide that you have given a section more prominence than it requires. In this instance, you would want to *demote* the section and make the heading one level lower. Once again, this is done in the Outline view. Suppose you want to demote the section headed <u>Dogs</u>. This is in fact a sub-section of <u>Any Other Business</u> and should not be a main section at all. To demote it:

    ↳ Display the headings to the appropriate level

    ↳ Select the heading

    ↳ Click the **Demote** button

There is one very important thing to remember. All sub-sections of the selected section will also be demoted unless they are displayed and not explicitly selected. The rules for selecting sections and sub-sections are:

    ↳ To demote a section *and* all its sub-sections, display the headings only to section level and select the section heading before clicking the **Demote** button

⌛ To demote just the section, and *not* its sub-sections, display the sub-sections and just select the main section heading before clicking the **Demote** button

To see how this works, display the headings down to level 3 and then select only the heading <u>Dogs</u>. This will mean that <u>Dogs</u> sub-section will be demoted, but the sub-section <u>Overhead Cables</u> will stay at the same level.

- If necessary, click the **Show Heading 3** button.

- Select the heading <u>Dogs</u>.

- Click the **Demote** button.

The selected heading is demoted and renumbered as a sub-section of <u>Any Other Business</u>. You will notice that it has taken on the formatting of the Heading 2 style. The heading <u>Overhead Cables</u> has also been renumbered but, because it was not selected, remains a Heading 3 heading.

```
  ✛  6  Yearbook
  ✛  7  Any Other Business
      ✛  7.1 Dogs
              ✛  7.1.1      Overhead cables
```

You will also notice that <u>Date of Next Meeting</u> has been renumbered as section 8; previously it was section 9.

Promoting a section

You may now be wondering why <u>Overhead Cables</u> is a sub-section of <u>Dogs</u>. Of course, this is also an item in <u>Any Other Business</u> and should be of equal importance to <u>Dogs</u>. This section needs to be promoted. To promote a section:

⌛ Display the headings to the appropriate level

⌛ Select the heading

⌛ Click the **Promote** button

There are two rules for selecting sections and sub-sections
- which are similar to those for demoting sections:

    🖎   To promote a section *and* all its sub-sections, display the headings only to section level and select the section heading before clicking the **Promote** button

    🖎   To promote just the section, and *not* its sub-sections, display the sub-sections and just select the section heading before clicking the **Promote** button

When a section is promoted, the heading will be renumbered and take on the style of the next heading level up. Try this out now.

●   Select the heading Overhead Cables.

●   Click the **Promote** button.

The section is promoted and the heading renumbered and reformatted, as shown in the next picture.

```
⇧  6  Yearbook
⇧  7  Any Other Business
        ⇧  7.1 Dogs
        ⇧  7.2 Overhead cables
```

Finishing off

To finish off, you need to return to look at the document in the Page Layout view and check the indentation of the sections you demoted and promoted. You will find that they are no longer correct.

●   Open the **View** menu and choose **Page Layout**, or click the **Page Layout View** button.

●   Click anywhere in the paragraph starting Dogs are still.

●   Click the **Increase Indent** button once.

The text is now aligned correctly with respect to its heading.

- Click anywhere in the paragraph starting <u>Visiting sailors</u>.

- Click the **Decrease Indent** button once.

The minutes are now complete and you can save and print them if you wish.

- If you wish, save the document on your exercise diskette, with the filename **a:My Minutes**.

- If you wish, print the document.

Inserting a table of contents

Sometimes when you write a report, you will want to insert a table of contents. Word provides the capability to do this with the **Index and Tables** option in the **Insert** menu. Although the **My Minutes** document is only short, you can try adding a table of contents at the end.

- Move the insertion point to the end of the document (**Ctrl+End**).

- Press **Enter** to move to the next page.

- Open the **Insert** menu and choose **Index and Tables**.

The Index and Tables dialog box is opened.

- If necessary, click the **Table of Contents** tab.

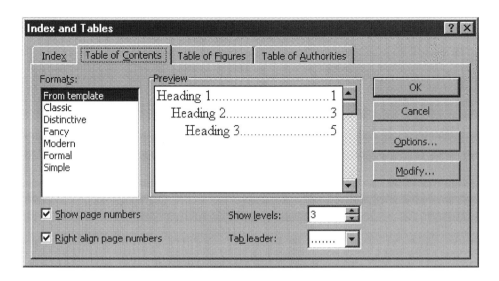

In this dialog box you can choose:

- ✎ A format for your contents list

- ✎ Whether or not to show page numbers

- ✎ Which heading levels to show

- ✎ Whether or not to right-align the page numbers

- ✎ The character for the tab leader between the text and right-aligned page numbers

The _Preview_ box will display the current options. Additional options can be obtained by clicking the **Options** and **Modify** buttons.

For this particular contents list, you will show two levels of heading, Heading 1 and Heading 2, and choose a continuous line as the tab leader.

- In the Formats list, check that **From template** is chosen.

- If necessary, click **Show page numbers** so that it is ticked.

- Change the entry in the Show levels box to **2**.

The _Preview_ box will now show just Headings 1 and 2.

- If necessary, click **Right align page numbers** so that it is ticked.

- Open the Tab leader list box and choose the continuous line (it is the last choice).

The tab leader in the <u>Preview</u> box will now be a continuous line.

● Click **OK**.

The contents list is inserted into your document at the insertion point.

1	Apologies	1
2	Minutes of Last Meeting	1
3	Matters Arising	1
	3.1 Road	1
	3.2 Beer Store	1
4	Reports	1
	4.1 Commodore - James Burston	1
	4.2 Treasurer - Catherine Rigby	1
	4.3 Secretary - Robert Maynard	2
	4.4 Sailing Secretary - Frank Wright	2
5	Newsletter	2
6	Yearbook	2
7	Any Other Business	2
	7.1 Dogs	2
	7.2 Overhead cables	2
8	Date of Next Meeting	2

Ending the session

You have now completed this chapter. You can either move on to the next chapter or exit Word. First, you should close the current document.

● Open the **File** menu and choose **Close** - when prompted, choose **No** to avoid saving the changes.

● If you are not continuing directly with the next chapter and want to stop now, open the **File** menu and choose **Exit** to exit Word.

Summary ~ Report Writing

Using styles

In the Normal template, Word provides a number of heading styles. To apply a style to a heading:

- ✏ Position the insertion point in the heading

- ✏ Open the **Style** list box and choose the appropriate style

Numbering headings

If a document is written using the heading styles provided in the Normal template, the headings can be numbered easily. Do as follows:

- ✏ Open the **Format** menu and choose **Bullets and Numbering**, and then click the **Outline Numbered** tab

- ✏ Choose the numbering style you require and click **OK**

 Use the **Increase Indent** button to indent the body text to match the heading and numbering style you have chosen.

Adding and inserting sub-headings

To add a sub-section beneath an existing section heading:

- ✏ Position the insertion point at the end of the main section heading and press **Enter**

- ✏ Open the **Style** list box and choose the appropriate style for the sub-heading

- ✏ Type the sub-heading

To insert a sub-section among existing sub-sections:

- ✏ Position the insertion point at the beginning of the sub-section heading before which you want to insert the sub-section

- ✏ Press **Enter**

↪ Type the sub-heading

Outline view

To display a document in the Outline view:

 ↪ Open the **View** menu and choose **Outline**, or click the **Outline View** button

The Outline view has a set of useful toolbar buttons which allow you to view and move sections of text by level.

 ↪ To display the complete document, click the **Show All Headings** button

 ↪ To display just the first line of body text, click the **Show First Line Only** button

 ↪ To display the headings down to a specific level, click the appropriate **Show Heading** button

 ↪ To display the formatting of the headings, click the **Show Formatting** button

 ↪ To expand/collapse a section to show/hide all sub-sections and body text, select the section heading and click the **Expand** button or the **Collapse** button once

 ↪ To expand/collapse a section one level at a time, click in the section heading and click the **Expand** button or the **Collapse** button once for each level to be expanded/collapsed

To move, promote or demote a section

↪ Display the headings to the appropriate level

↪ Select the section heading

↪ Click the **Move Up**, **Move Down**, **Promote** or **Demote** button as appropriate

The rules for moving/promoting/demoting sections are:

- ✎ To move/promote/demote a section *and* all its sub-sections, display the headings only to section level and select the section heading before clicking the appropriate button

- ✎ To move/promote/demote just the section, *not* its sub-sections, display the sub-sections and just select the main section heading before clicking the appropriate button

Inserting a table of contents

- ✎ Position the insertion point where you would like to place the table of contents

- ✎ Open the **Insert** menu and choose **Index and Tables**, and then click the **Table of Contents** tab

- ✎ Choose a format for the table of contents

- ✎ Choose the options you require, e.g., heading levels to be shown, page numbers to be shown, tab leaders, etc.

- ✎ Click **OK**, or press **Enter**

Notes

Use this page to make notes of your own.

Page #   Notes

_____   _____

_____   _____

_____   _____

_____   _____

_____   _____

_____   _____

_____   _____

_____   _____

_____   _____

_____   _____

_____   _____

_____   _____

_____   _____

_____   _____

Notes

Use this page to make notes of your own.

Page #   Notes

_____   _____

_____   _____

_____   _____

_____   _____

_____   _____

_____   _____

_____   _____

_____   _____

_____   _____

_____   _____

_____   _____

_____   _____

_____   _____

_____   _____

_____   _____

Chapter 9 ~ Managing Files

The Open and Save As dialog boxes provide a number of useful features for managing files. *Searching for Files* is covered in the next chapter.

In this chapter you will learn about:

    ✎   Document properties

    ✎   Document statistics

    ✎   Saving documents to the hard drive

    ✎   Creating new folders

    ✎   Adding shortcuts to Favorites

    ✎   Using Favorites to open files

    ✎   Inserting a file

    ✎   Sending documents to the A drive

    ✎   Renaming and deleting documents

    ✎   Deleting folders and shortcuts

    ✎   Working with groups of files

Getting started

- If necessary, start your Word program.

- If the Office Assistant is displayed at any time throughout this chapter, you should read what it has to say and then close it – click the **Close** button in the Office Assistant window.

You should be starting with a new blank document.

- If necessary, click the **New** button to open a new document.

Document properties

When you save a document, Word automatically saves some general information for you. This will include document statistics like file size, the dates the document was created and last modified, the number of words and so on. You can also enter information that will make the document easier to find if you forget its filename: a descriptive title, keywords, the subject, etc. Some of this information is displayed when you have the Properties view chosen in the Open or Save As dialog boxes.

The user information is entered in the Properties dialog box. This may be displayed each time you save a file for the first time, but this option is often switched off and the dialog box is not displayed. You will start by setting the option to display the Properties dialog box.

●   Open the **Tools** menu and choose **Options**.

The Options dialog box is displayed.

●   Click the **Save** tab.

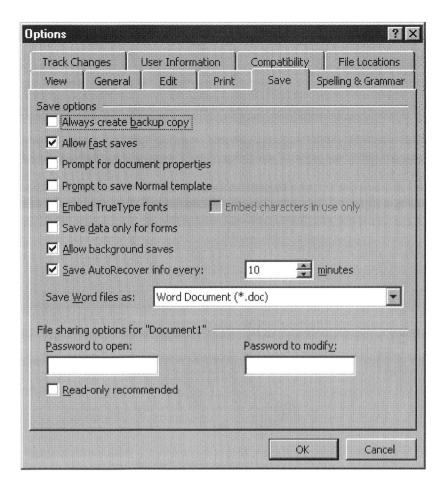

- Click the **Prompt for document properties** option so that it is ticked.

- Click **OK**, or press **Enter**.

Now enter some text in the new document and save it.

- Type the heading:

  Managing Files

- Press **Enter** twice and then type:

  This document will be used to demonstrate various file management features.

You need to save the file to your exercise diskette.

- Open the **File** menu and choose **Save**, or click the **Save** button, or press **Ctrl+S**.

- If necessary, open the <u>Look in</u> list box and choose **3½ Floppy (A:)**.

The <u>File name</u> box will already display the heading from your document. You can use this for the document name.

● Click **Save,** or press **Enter.**

The document Properties dialog box is displayed.

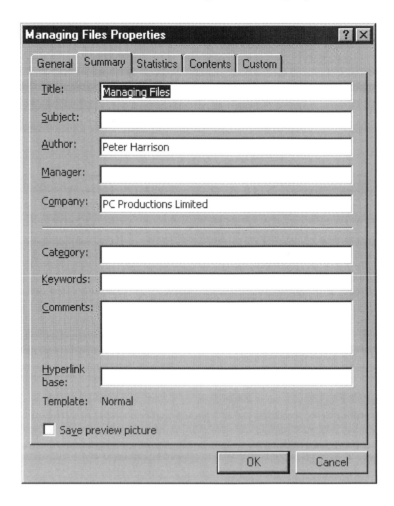

You can type any information you like in the appropriate boxes.

> ✦ *If your name is not shown as the author, you can change it for this document only by selecting the entry and typing your own name. To change the author for all documents you should change the entry in the* <u>*Name*</u> *box in **Tools**, **Options**, **User Information**.*

● Add any information you wish.

● When you are ready, click **OK,** or press **Enter.**

The document is saved with the filename **Managing Files**.

Viewing document properties

There are three ways to open the Properties dialog box and view this summary information, depending on where you are at the time.

    ✎   If the document is open already, open the **File** menu and choose **Properties**

    ✎   If you are in the Open or Save As dialog boxes, right-click the document name and choose **Properties** in the shortcut menu

    ✎   Also in the Open or Save As dialog boxes, click the document name, click the **Commands and Settings** button and choose **Properties** in the shortcut menu

As you have the document open already, you can use the first method this time.

●   Open the **File** menu and choose **Properties**.

The Properties dialog box is displayed. You could change this information if you wished by selecting the item and typing any new information.

Document statistics

When you saved the document, Word also saved information about the file. To view this, click the **Statistics** tab in the Properties dialog box.

●   Click the **Statistics** tab.

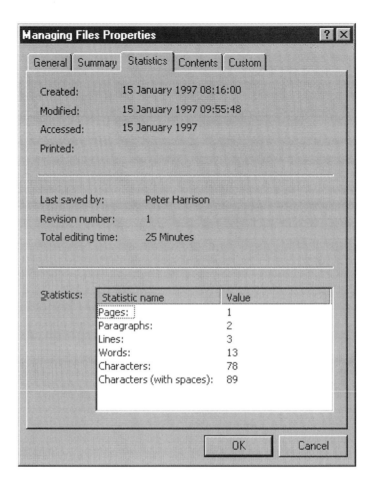

- Read through the information presented and then click **Cancel**, or press **Esc**, to close the dialog box.

Printing document properties

You can print some of the document properties. To do this:

- ✎ Open the Print dialog box (**File**, **Print**)

- ✎ Open the Print what list box and choose **Document properties**

- ✎ Click **OK**, or press **Enter**

Try this now:

- Open the **File** menu and choose **Print**, or press **Ctrl+P**.

- Open the Print what list box and choose **Document properties**.

- Click OK, or press Enter.

The summary information for the **Managing Files** document is printed.

Saving documents to the hard drive

So far on this course, you have saved documents only to the exercise diskette. However, in your everyday work, you will probably store documents on your hard disk. Your hard disk is divided into folders. The default folder assigned by Word is **My Documents**.

If you create few documents, this folder will probably be suitable for your needs. However, if you create a large number of documents, or share a machine with someone else, you will need to organise your documents in other folders or sub-folders. You can create sub-folders within My Documents, or create additional folders on your hard drive. This is not as difficult as it sounds. Word provides a **Create New Folder** button in the Save As dialog box.

You can try this out now, by saving the **Managing Files** document to a new sub-folder called **Advanced Courseware**, in the My Documents folder.

Creating a new folder

To create a new folder easily, you need to open the Save As dialog box.

- Open the **File** menu and choose **Save As**.

- Open the Save in list box and click the icon for drive **C**.

- Double-click the **My Documents** folder icon to open the folder.

This folder may be completely empty, or it may contain folders or files created previously.

- Click the **Create New Folder** button.

The New Folder dialog box is displayed. The name <u>New</u>
<u>Folder</u> is suggested in the <u>Name</u> box. Because it is
highlighted, you can just type a new name.

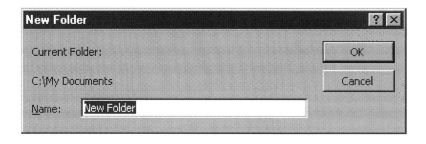

- In the <u>Name</u> box, type:

  Advanced Courseware

- Click **OK,** or press **Enter.**

The new folder is now shown in the folders list for the My
Documents folder. To save the document to this folder, it
must first be opened. You can then save the document
with a new name, **Managing Files 2**.

- Double-click the icon for the **Advanced
  Courseware** folder.

- Change the entry in the <u>File name</u> box to:

  Managing Files 2

- Click **Save,** or press **Enter.**

Once again the Properties dialog box will be displayed.

- Click the **Summary** tab and make any changes
  you wish.

- When you are ready, click **OK,** or press
  Enter.

The document is saved to your hard drive. The name in
the Title bar changes to <u>Managing Files 2</u>. You can now
close this document.

- Close the **Managing Files 2** document.

Favorites

Windows provides a folder called **Favorites** in which you can store shortcuts to any folders or files you use frequently. In Word, there is a shortcut stored in Favorites which leads to the My Documents folder. To access this shortcut, you have to click the **Look in Favorites** button in the Open or Save As dialog boxes. As usual, the best way to learn is by example.

- Open the **File** menu and choose **Open,** or
  click the **Open** button, or
  press **Ctrl+O.**

The Open dialog box is displayed.

- Click the **Look in Favorites** button.

The Favorites folder is displayed in the <u>Look in</u> box and the shortcut to My Documents is shown in the list of shortcuts. If the shortcut is not shown, you will have to create the shortcut yourself.

- If the **My Documents** shortcut is not shown,
  open the <u>Look in</u> list box and click the
  icon for drive **C.**

- Click **My Documents.**

- Click the **Add to Favorites** button and
  choose **Add Selected Item to Favorites.**

- Click the **Look in Favorites** button to
  return to the Favorites folder.

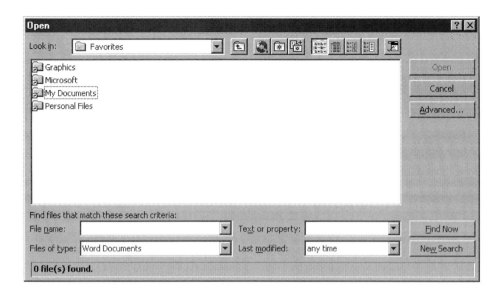

To open the My Documents folder, just double-click the shortcut:

- Double-click the shortcut icon for **My Documents**.

The My Documents folder is opened and the **Advanced Courseware** folder you created earlier is displayed in the folders list.

Adding to Favorites

It is easy to add a shortcut for any folder or file. This can be done in the Open dialog box:

- ✎ Use the Look in list box to locate the appropriate folder

- ✎ Select the file(s) you want a shortcut to

- ✎ Click the **Add to Favorites** button

- ✎ Choose whether to add the complete folder or just the selected file(s)

You can try this out now by adding shortcuts for two files on the exercise diskette.

- If necessary, click the **Open** button.

- Open the Look in list box and choose **3½ Floppy (A:)**.

The list of documents on the exercise diskette is displayed. You will choose two of these: **Birthdays** and **Orville Wright**.

- Choose the document **Birthdays**.

- Hold down the **Ctrl** key and choose **Orville Wright**.

- Click the **Add to Favorites** button.

A small menu is displayed. In this instance you want to add the selected items, not the complete contents of the exercise diskette in drive A.

> A̲dd '3½ Floppy (A:)' to Favorites
> A̲dd Selected Items to Favorites

- Choose **Add Selected Items to Favorites**.

The appropriate shortcuts are now ready for you to use.

Using Favorites to open files

The shortcuts that you have set up in Favorites can be used to open files from the Open dialog box. The same links are also available in other dialog boxes, for example, Insert File and Insert Picture; you just click the **Look in Favorites** button and the Favorites folder is opened.

To check that the shortcuts have been set up, click the **Look in Favorites** button and open the **Orville Wright** document.

- Click the **Look in Favorites** button.

The Look in box displays the Favorites folder again. You should now find the **Birthdays** and the **Orville Wright** documents in the list of Favorites.

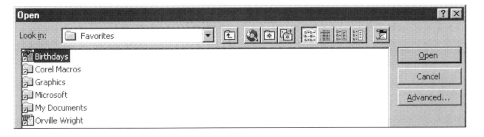

- Double-click the shortcut icon for the **Orville Wright** document.

The document is opened from your exercise diskette.

> ♪ *The actual file is not moved to the Favorites folder. The file remains in its original place and is accessed via a shortcut stored in Favorites.*

Inserting a file

There may sometimes be an instance when you want to combine the current document with another one. This is done using the **Insert**, **File** menu option. The file is always inserted at the insertion point. You can try this out now by inserting the **Birthdays** document at the end of the current document.

- Move the insertion point to the end of the document (**Ctrl+End**).

- Press **Enter** twice.

- Open the **Insert** menu and choose **File**.

The Insert File dialog box is opened. Note that this is very similar to the Open dialog box, with the same toolbar of useful buttons, including a **Look in Favorites** button that you can use to help you open the **Birthdays** document.

- If necessary, click the **Look in Favorites** button.

- Double-click the shortcut icon for the **Birthdays** document.

After a short while, the chosen document is inserted at the insertion point. You can now close the document.

- Close the **Orville Wright** document – choose **No** to avoid saving the changes.

Using the right-hand mouse button

The right-hand mouse button can be used to manage files in the Open or Save As dialog boxes. As you might expect, it accesses a shortcut menu of useful options. To investigate these options you need to have one of the dialog boxes open.

- Click the **Open** button to display the Open dialog box.

- Open the Look in list box and choose 3½ **Floppy (A:)**.

- Right-click the document **European Populations** and view the options in the shortcut menu.

The options available are listed and explained in the following table:

Option	Description
Open	Opens the selected file(s).
Open Read-Only	Opens the selected file(s) as read only, i.e. the opened file(s) cannot be edited and saved to the same name.
Open as Copy	Opens a copy of the selected file(s). The copy is automatically named and saved into the same folder as the original.
Print	Prints the selected file(s).
Send To	Sends a copy of the selected file(s) to either drive A, the Briefcase on the Windows Desktop, or a Mail Recipient (if available).
Cut	Removes the selected file(s) to the Windows Clipboard.
Copy	Copies the selected file(s) to the Windows Clipboard.
Create Shortcut	Creates a shortcut for the selected file(s).
Delete	Deletes the selected file(s).
Rename	Renames the selected file.
Properties	Displays the Properties dialog box for the selected file(s).

Right-clicking a file, or a group of files, in the Save As dialog box produces a similar list of options. However, the **Open**, **Open Read-Only** and **Open as Copy** options are replaced by a **Save** option; all the other options are the same.

Printing a document without opening it

If you choose **Print** from the shortcut menu the document is printed without being opened. You can try this out now.

● Right-click **European Populations** and choose **Print**.

After a short pause the **European Populations** document is printed.

Sending documents to the A drive

The **Send To** option is very useful for copying documents from your hard drive to a diskette in drive A. You can also use the option to send files to the Briefcase on the Windows Desktop, or to a Mail recipient if you are using Microsoft Outlook.

To try this out, you can copy the document from the Advanced Courseware folder to your exercise diskette.

- Click the **Open** button.

- Click the **Look in Favorites** button.

- Double-click the shortcut icon for **My Documents**.

- Double-click the **Advanced Courseware** folder.

- Right-click **Managing Files 2**.

- In the shortcut menu, point to **Send To** and choose **3½ Floppy (A)**.

The document is copied onto the exercise diskette.

Renaming documents

The shortcut menu can also be used to rename files. Just right-click the file and choose **Rename**. The document name is highlighted and you can type the new name straight away. Try renaming the **Managing Files 2** document.

- Right-click **Managing Files 2** and choose **Rename**.

- Type:

  Renamed File

- Press **Enter**.

The file is renamed accordingly.

Deleting documents

Documents can be deleted from the file list in the Open dialog box by right-clicking the filename and choosing **Delete**. You can try this out now by deleting the **Renamed File** from the Advanced Courseware folder.

- Right-click **Renamed File** and choose **Delete**.

Word displays a message box asking you to confirm that you want to send the file to the Recycle Bin. The file is sent to the Recycle Bin and not deleted permanently because it was saved to your hard disk, not the exercise diskette. If you needed to restore it, you could, as long as the Recycle Bin was not emptied and the file permanently deleted as a result.

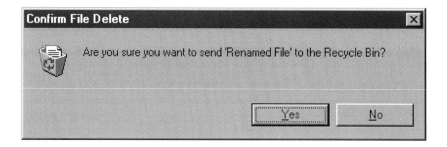

- Choose **Yes** to send the file to the Recycle Bin.

The document is deleted from the Advanced Courseware folder.

Deleting a folder

Folders can be deleted in the same way as files. Just right-click any folder in the folder list and choose delete. You can delete the Advanced Courseware folder next. However, you have to move to the next folder up first, so that the Advanced Courseware folder can be right-clicked in the folders list.

- Click the **Up One Level** button.

- In the folders list, right-click **Advanced Courseware** and choose **Delete**.

- Choose **Yes** to confirm the deletion.

Deleting shortcuts

Before finishing this section, you need to delete the two shortcuts you added to Favorites. You can also do this in the Open dialog box.

- If necessary, click the **Open** button.

- Click the **Look in Favorites** button.

As you might expect, you can choose multiple items for deletion by using the **Ctrl** key. You can then right-click the selection and choose the option you require from the shortcut menu. Try this now. Delete the shortcuts for **Birthdays** and **Orville Wright**.

- Click the shortcut icon for the **Birthdays** document.

- Hold down the **Ctrl** key and click the shortcut icon for the **Orville Wright** document.

- Right-click one of the selected items and choose **Delete**.

Word displays a message box asking you to confirm that these two items should be sent to the Recycle Bin. Although the message box is called Confirm Multiple File Delete, it is only the *shortcuts* that are being sent to the Recycle Bin, not the documents themselves. The documents will still be on the exercise diskette.

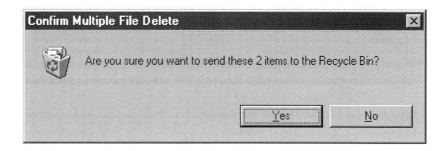

- Choose **Yes** to confirm the deletion.

You can now check that the two documents are still on the exercise diskette.

- If necessary, click the **Open** button.

- Open the <u>Look in</u> list box, and choose 3½ **Floppy (A:)**.

You will see that the **Birthdays** and **Orville Wright** documents are still in the list of files. You can also confirm that the **Managing Files 2** document, which you sent to the A drive earlier, is on the exercise diskette.

Inspecting document properties

As mentioned earlier, you can inspect the properties for any document listed in the Open or Save As dialog boxes. You can do this now for the **Managing Files 2** document.

● Locate and right-click **Managing Files 2**.

● In the shortcut menu, choose **Properties**.

The Managing Files 2 Properties dialog box is displayed.

● When you are ready, click **OK,** or press **Enter** to close the Properties dialog box.

Working with groups of files

When you have a large number of files it is often useful to be able to sort them, or search for, a particular file or group of files. The options for searching are covered in the chapter *Searching for Files*.

Sorting

Sorting allows you to change the order of the document files displayed. If you have followed the *Microsoft Word 97 Intermediate* course you will be familiar with the sort options provided in the Details view. Switch to the Details view now.

● Click the **Details** button.

● Click the **Size** button to order the files, smallest first.

● Click the **Modified** button to order the files with the most recent file first.

You can also change the order of the files in any of the other three views. Similar sort options are provided using the **Sorting** option in the **Commands and Settings** shortcut menu.

- Click the **List** button.

- Click the **Commands and Settings** button, and then choose **Sorting** in the shortcut menu.

The Sort By dialog box is opened.

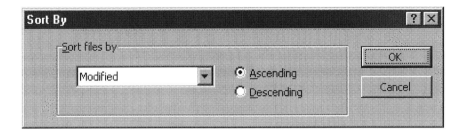

The <u>Sort files by</u> options allow you to sort the list of files displayed in different ways, by filename, size, type of file or last modified date.

- Open the <u>Sort files by</u> list box and choose **Size**.

- Click the **Descending** option so that it is chosen.

- Click **OK**, or press **Enter**.

The new list is presented. You can now change it back so the files are ordered by ascending filename.

- Click the **Commands and Settings** button, and then choose **Sorting** in the shortcut menu.

- Open the <u>Sort files by</u> list box and choose **Name**.

- Click the **Ascending** option so that it is chosen.

- Click **OK**, or press **Enter**.

Selecting multiple files

You will have already gathered that groups of files can be selected and then managed as a group. The options in the shortcut menu can apply to groups of files, as well as single files.

To choose a file, just click it. To choose more than one file, hold down the **Ctrl** key and click the individual files. To choose a list of files, click the first file, hold down the **Shift** key and click the last file in the list.

- Make sure no files are currently selected.

- Hold down the **Ctrl** key and click the **Birthdays, European Populations, Sorting** and **Worry** documents.

---
*If you select the wrong file, you can de-select it by clicking it again (still with **Ctrl** depressed).*

- De-select the **Worry** document you have just selected.

Once you have selected the files you want to work with, you can use the options available in the shortcut menu, for example, open, print, copy, cut or delete.

Printing a group of files

- Right-click any of the selected files and choose **Print.**

The selected files are printed.

Copy and Cut options

Once you have chosen a group of files, you can either copy or move them to another existing folder, or drive, using the **Copy** or **Cut** options in the shortcut menu. Try moving two files from your exercise diskette to the My Documents folder on drive C (you will delete them again afterwards). This involves using **Cut** to remove them from the exercise diskette, and **Paste** to save them onto the hard drive.

- Click the **Open** button to display the Open dialog box.

- Choose the document **Managing Files 2.**

- Hold down the **Ctrl** key and choose the document **Managing Files.**

- Right-click the selection and choose **Cut.**

You now need to locate the My Documents folder. You can look in Favorites.

- Click the **Look in Favorites** button.

The shortcut to the My Documents folder is shown in the folder list. All you need to do is right-click the shortcut name and choose **Paste**. The two documents will then be moved into this folder.

- Right-click **My Documents** and choose **Paste**.

Word displays a message box showing that each file is being moved from the A drive to My Documents.

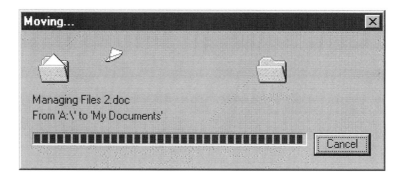

- Double-click the shortcut icon for **My Documents**.

The folder is opened and the two files are now shown. You can now delete them.

Deleting groups of files

You have already deleted two shortcuts together. A group of files is deleted in the same way. You will try deleting two files this time.

- Select both document files – **Managing Files 2** and **Managing Files**.

- Right-click the selection and choose **Delete**.

- Choose **Yes** to confirm the deletion.

- Click **Cancel,** or press **Esc,** to close the Open dialog box.

Finishing off

To finish off this chapter, you should change the option that automatically displays the Properties dialog box when you save a file for the first time back to its original setting.

- If there are no documents open, click the **New** button.

- Open the **Tools** menu and choose **Options**.

- If necessary, click the **Save** tab.

- Click the **Prompt for document properties** option so that it is not ticked.

- Click **OK**, or press **Enter**.

Ending the session

You have now completed the tutorial in this chapter. You can either move on to the next chapter or exit Word. First, you should close any document you have open.

- Open the **File** menu and choose **Close** – if asked, choose **No** to avoid saving any changes.

- If you are not continuing directly with the next chapter and want to stop now, open the **File** menu and choose **Exit** to exit Word.

Summary ~ Managing Files

Document properties

When you first save a document, you can enter information in the Properties dialog box. To display the Properties dialog box each time you save a new document:

- ⮡ Open the **Tools** menu and choose **Options**

- ⮡ Click the **Save** tab

- ⮡ Click **Prompt for document properties** so that it is ticked

Document statistics

These are saved by Word each time you save a document. To view them:

- ᪥ When the document is open, open the **File** menu and choose **Properties**

- ᪥ In the Open or Save As dialog boxes, right-click the document name and choose **Properties**

Creating a new folder

- ᪥ In the Save As dialog box, use the <u>Save in</u> list box to open the folder or drive where you want the new folder to be

- ᪥ Click the **Create New Folder** button

- ᪥ Type a name for the folder

Adding shortcuts to Favorites

To add a shortcut to Favorites, open the Open dialog box and then:

- ᪥ Choose the file(s) to which you want a shortcut

- ᪥ Click the **Add to Favorites** button

- ᪥ Choose whether to add the individual file(s) or the whole folder

Using Favorites to open files

To open a file with a shortcut in Favorites:

- ᪥ Click the **Open** button

- ᪥ Click the **Look in Favorites** button

- ᪥ Double-click the shortcut for the file you want to open

Inserting a file

To insert a file at the insertion point:

- ✥ Open the **Insert** menu and choose **File**

- ✥ In the Insert File dialog box, locate the file and double-click it

Using the right-hand mouse button

In the Open and Save As dialog boxes, you can use the right-hand mouse button to access a number of options for a particular file or group of files. To select a group of files:

- ✥ Click the first file

- ✥ Hold down the **Ctrl** key and click the other files in turn

Then use the right-hand mouse button for file management as follows:

Open	Opens the selected file(s).
Open Read-Only	Opens the selected file(s) as read only i.e., the opened file(s) cannot be edited and saved to the same name.
Open as Copy	Creates, and opens a copy of the selected file(s).
Print	Prints the selected file(s).
Send To	Sends a copy of the selected file(s) to either drive A, the Briefcase on the Windows Desktop, or a Mail Recipient (if available).
Cut	Removes the selected file(s) to the Windows Clipboard.
Copy	Copies the selected file(s) to the Windows Clipboard.
Create Shortcut	Creates a shortcut for the selected file(s).
Delete	Deletes the selected file(s).
Rename	Renames the selected file(s).
Properties	Displays the Properties dialog box for the selected file(s).

Sorting files

Files can be sorted in Details view in the Open and Save As dialog boxes, by clicking the appropriate buttons. To sort them in the other views:

    ↳   Click the **Commands and Settings** button

    ↳   Choose **Sorting**, then choose the options you require

Notes

Use this page to make notes of your own.

Page #   Notes

_____   _____

_____   _____

_____   _____

_____   _____

_____   _____

_____   _____

_____   _____

_____   _____

_____   _____

_____   _____

_____   _____

_____   _____

_____   _____

_____   _____

_____   _____

_____   _____

Chapter 10 ~ Searching for Files

The Open dialog box provides several features that help you to search for files. The Look in list box enables you to choose the drive and folder you wish to search. Additionally, there are four simple search criteria you can set and then a wide range of advanced criteria you can choose, to narrow a search further.

In this chapter you will learn about:

- ✎ Choosing drives and folders
- ✎ Changing drives
- ✎ Opening and changing folders
- ✎ Searching by filename or file type
- ✎ Searching by text or property
- ✎ Searching by date last modified
- ✎ Defining an advanced search
- ✎ Saving a search
- ✎ Searching for a document by number of words
- ✎ Using a saved search
- ✎ Opening a search
- ✎ Editing a search
- ✎ Deleting searches

To get started

● If necessary, start your Word program.

- If the Office Assistant is displayed at any time throughout this chapter, you should read what it has to say and then close it – click the **Close** button in the Office Assistant window.

Drives and folders

If you have a large number of files or documents, it is not always possible to remember all their names or even where they are stored. You should always remember that although your computer is an admirable piece of equipment, it is not intelligent and is completely incapable of working on its own initiative. If, therefore, you wish to load a document you have named **Worth**, but can only remember that it was called something that began with 'W', the computer cannot do it alone. If you try to retrieve a document called 'W', the computer does not have the intelligence to understand what you really want.

Sometimes you may find it difficult to find a document that you know *does* exist. This will happen if your document has been saved in one folder or drive, but you are searching in another.

- Open the **File** menu and choose **Open**, or click the **Open** button, or press **Ctrl+O**.

The Open dialog box is displayed. This should now be thoroughly familiar to you! A list of documents available in the current drive and folder is displayed.

Changing drives

To change drives, just open the <u>Look in</u> list box and choose the desired drive.

- Make sure your exercise diskette is in drive A.

- Open the <u>Look in</u> list box and choose **3½ Floppy (A:)**.

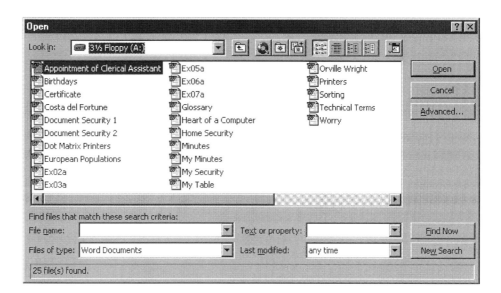

- Open the <u>Look in</u> list box and click the icon for your C: drive **(C:)**.

A number of folders and files are now shown in the box below the <u>Look in</u> list box. These will include the **My Documents** folder you have used previously.

Opening and changing folders

Each hard disk drive has its own set of folders. The list of folders in each drive can be displayed by clicking the icon for that drive.

To open a folder, double-click its icon.

- Double-click the icon for the **My Documents** folder.

The list of files may or may not be empty.

- Click the **Up One Level** button to move back up to drive C.

- Try double-clicking a few more folders in the folder list.

Simple file searches

It is very easy to get Word to list only specific groups of files. This is especially useful when the number of files has grown, so that using the scroll boxes to locate files becomes tedious.

●   `Open the` <u>`Look in`</u> `list box and choose` **3½ Floppy (A:).**

The documents on your exercise diskette will be listed again. Normally, Word lists all the files in the current folder that are Word documents. However, you can list other files, or specific groups of files.

At the bottom of the Open dialog box are the <u>Find files that match these criteria</u> group of options. There are four simple criteria that can be used to search for and list files in the current folder. These are:

    ↳   File name

    ↳   Files of type

    ↳   Text or property

    ↳   Last modified

As you are probably familiar with the first two criteria, you can try them out now.

Searching by filename

To search by filename, you should type the filename in the <u>File name</u> box. However, if you can only remember the first letter or two of the filename, you can use an asterisk * in place of the rest of the filename. The asterisk * is commonly referred to as a *wildcard*.

The following table will help to explain what is meant.

Filename with wildcard	Description
.	Any file with any extension, i.e., all files.
*.doc	Any file with the extension .doc.
Birthdays.*	Any file with the name Birthdays and any extension.
Birthdays.doc	Any file with the name Birthdays and the extension .doc, i.e., the file Birthdays.doc.
B*.doc	Any file starting with B with the extension .doc.
B*.*	Any file starting with B, with any extension.

With this knowledge, we can make listing files much more comprehensible.

- Click the File name box to move the insertion point there.

- Type:

  s*

- Check the Files of type box reads **Word Documents**.

- Click **Find Now**.

While the search is taking place, the **Find Now** button changes to a **Stop** button. This can be used to stop the search at any time. In this instance, if the search is very quick, you may not even notice the change.

The list of files is updated to include only those starting with s that are Word documents. There will be at least one file - **Sorting**.

Searching by file type

The Files of type list box is used to specify the *type* of files you want to search for and open.

- Open the Files of type list box.

There will be a list of file types displayed that you can scroll down. The exact contents will depend on the options that were chosen when Word was installed on your computer.

- Scroll the list of file types to see what is available.

- Click the **All Files** option.

The list of files is updated again to include another file that begins with s, **Spain**. This is a bitmap image, not a Word document.

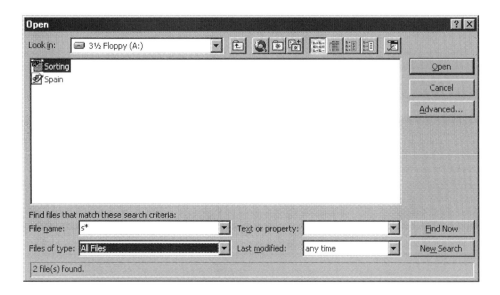

You will have noticed that most of the file type options are for files from word processing applications. You can open any file whose type is listed in the <u>Files of type</u> list box. However, if you know the extension for other files you want to look for, you can use the wildcard system explained earlier. Try this out now, by searching for all the Windows Metafiles on the exercise diskette. These are picture files used in this course and have the extension **.wmf**. To insert any of these files into a document, you would of course use the **Insert**, **Picture** option. Here, in the Open dialog box, you are just investigating a way of searching for files with a different extension.

- Click the **New Search** button to clear the existing search criteria.

- In the <u>File name</u> box, type:

  *.wmf

- Click **Find Now**.

Once again, while Word searches for the files, the **Find Now** button will change to a **Stop** button. After a short while, three Windows Metafiles are listed - **Flyace.wmf**, **Houses.wmf** and **Leaves.wmf**.

Text or property

Sometimes, you may want to search for a particular phrase that you remember writing, or you might want to review a number of documents containing a specific word. You may also recall using a particular phrase in the properties of a document, but you cannot recall which document it was. You can search for this phrase or word using the Text or property box.

- Click the **New Search** button to clear the previous search criteria.

- Click the Text or property box to move the insertion point there.

- Type:

  home

- Click **Find Now**.

Word will now look for all files on your exercise diskette with the word 'home' in their texts. This search will take longer than the previous searches and you should now see the **Stop** button in place of the **Find Now** button. You can use this button to stop a search whenever necessary. For example, you may have chosen to search such a large collection of files that the search is taking rather a long time; or the file you are looking for may have been found already.

The list of files is updated to show all those with the word 'home' in them. There will be at least five of them.

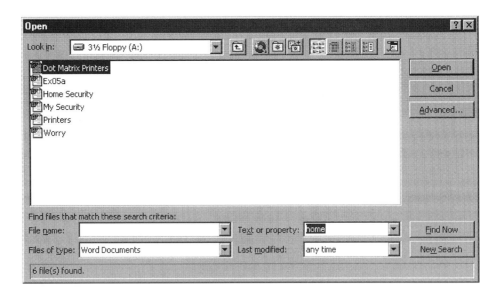

If you don't believe this, open one of the files and use the Find function to search for the word 'home'.

- Double-click the filename **Dot Matrix Printers**.

- When the document is opened, open the **Edit** menu and choose **Find,** or press **Ctrl+F.**

- In the Find what box, type:

  home

- Click **Find Next,** or press **Enter.**

Word will find the first occurrence of the word home in this document.

- Click **Cancel,** or press **Esc,** to close the Find and Replace dialog box.

- Close the **Dot Matrix Printers** document.

Last modified

The final simple search criterion is provided by the Last modified list box. You can use this to specify when the files were last modified.

- Click the **Open** button, or press **Ctrl+O** to display the Open dialog box.

- Open the Last modified list box.

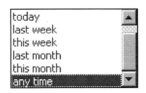

There are seven options; the default is **any time**. You can try the Last modified search criterion now.

- If you have saved some files earlier in the week, choose **this week** in the Last modified list box.

The list of files will be updated to show only those files on the exercise diskette that you have saved this week.

- Click the **New Search** button to reset the search criteria to the default settings.

Search the Web

In the Open dialog box toolbar, there is a **Search the Web** button. You can only use this if you have an Internet Browser, and are connected to the Internet.

🖰 Click the **Search the Web** button to display the search page of your Internet Browser

You will not be doing this now.

Advanced searches

The four basic search criteria may not always be sufficient to narrow down the searches you wish to execute. The Advanced Find dialog box can be used to specify more selective search criteria.

- In the Open dialog box, click the **Advanced** button.

The Advanced Find dialog box is opened. It has one search criterion already specified - Files of type is *All Files* or Files of type is *Word Documents*.

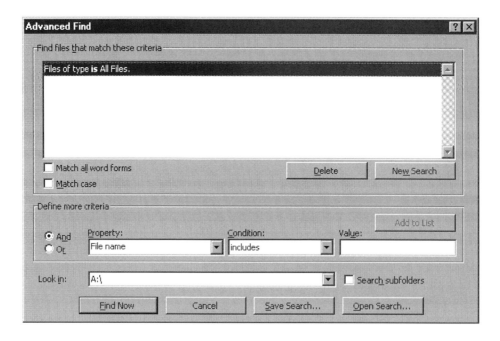

The Advanced Find dialog box allows you to tell Word what to look for and where to look. You can save individual searches and use them again.

- ✋ All search criteria that are currently specified, are displayed in the <u>Find files that match these criteria</u> box.

- ✋ To delete one of these criteria, click it to select it, then click the **Delete** button.

- ✋ To clear all the search criteria, and use the default values, click the **New Search** button.

- ✋ The **Match all word forms** and **Match case** options are used when searching for specific words or phrases, in the same way as you would use them in the Find function.

- ✋ The <u>Define more criteria</u> options let you add more search criteria to the <u>Find files that match these criteria</u> box. There are three settings to define:

  - ✋ <u>Property</u> - File name, Author, Number of words, etc.
  <u>Condition</u> - includes, less than, more than, etc.
  <u>Value</u> - type what you require in the box.

- ✎ These criteria can either be **And** or **Or**. Once you have defined a particular criterion, click **Add to List**.

- ✎ The Look in list box lets you choose a drive and folder. If the Search subfolders box is not ticked, only the chosen folder is searched. If it is ticked, all the sub-folders beneath the chosen folder are also searched.

- ✎ To start the search, click **Find Now**.

- ✎ To save the search, click **Save Search** and enter a name in the Save Search dialog box.

- ✎ To open a search, click **Open Search** and choose a search from the Open Search dialog box.

All these options may make the Advanced Find dialog box seem rather complicated. So, as usual, the best way to learn is by example.

Defining an advanced search

You are now going to define a search with two parameters:

- ✎ File type - Word document

- ✎ Author - Peter Harrison

First, if the existing search criterion is Files of type is *All Files*, you have to delete the criterion. However, if the existing search criterion is Files of type is *Word Documents*, you can skip the next four instructions.

- ● If necessary, click the **Files of type is All Files** criterion and click the **Delete** button.

- ● If necessary, open the Property list box and choose **Files of type**.

- ● Open the Condition list box and choose **Word Documents**.

- ● Click **Add to List**.

Now add the criterion for the author, Peter Harrison. As you want to add this to the previous criterion so that both apply to each file, you need to use the **And** option.

- Make sure the **And** option is chosen.

- Open the Property list box and choose **Author**.

- Open the Condition list box and choose **includes words**.

- In the Value box, type:

  Peter Harrison

- Click **Add to List**.

The two search criteria are now displayed in the Find files that match these criteria box.

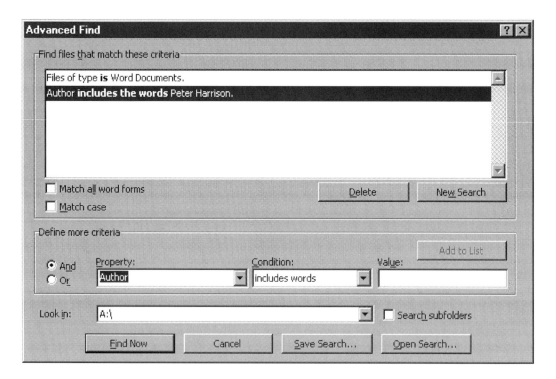

Before starting the search, you need to check that you are going to search the correct drive and/or folder. In this particular instance, you are going to search the exercise diskette in drive A. This diskette has no subfolders.

- If necessary, open the Look in list box, and choose **3½ Floppy (A:)**.

- Check that the **Search subfolders** option is not ticked.

All you have to do now is to start the search.

● Click **Find Now**.

You are returned to the Open dialog box. Word will keep track of how many files it has found so far, displaying the count in the Status bar at the bottom of the dialog box. Word will then list the files it has found. If you think the search is taking rather too long, you could always click the **Stop** button to stop the search.

After a while, four files are displayed in the list of files - **Appointment of a Clerical Assistant** and **Home Security**, together with the **Ex02a** and **My Security** (if you have completed Chapters 2 and 7). In the Status bar, Word tells you that four files have been found. Note that Word also indicates that the search criteria include those in Advanced Find.

Word indicates
additional
criteria
specified in
Advanced Find

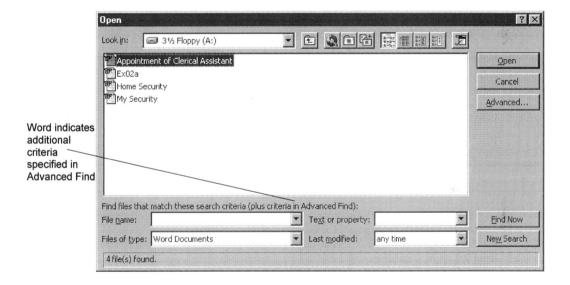

Saving a search

If you decide that you are likely to use a particular search again, you can save it. You need to have the Advanced Find dialog box open to do this.

● Click the **Advanced** button.

● In the Advanced Find dialog box, click **Save Search**.

The Save Search dialog box is opened. You just need to give the search a name, and then click **OK**, or press **Enter**.

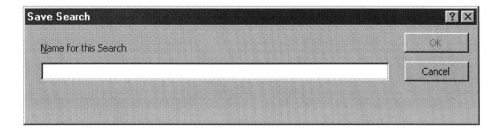

- In the Name for this Search box, type:

  Word docs by PH

- Click **OK**, or press **Enter**.

The search is now saved and you can create another one.

Searching for a document by number of words

There are many properties you can choose to search by, either separately or in conjunction with others.

- Click the **New Search** button.

- Open the Property list box and view the alternatives offered.

This time you can try searching by the number of words in a document.

- In the Property list box, choose **Number of words**.

- Open the Condition list box and choose **more than**.

- In the Value box, type:

  250

- Click **Add to List**.

This time, save the search before you run it:

- Click **Save Search**.

- In the Name for this Search box, type:

  More than 250 words

- Click **OK**, or press **Enter**.

Now proceed with the search.

- Click **Find Now**.

After a while, Word will find at least six documents that match these criteria: **Costa del Fortune**, **Dot Matrix Printers**, **Heart of a Computer**, **Printers**, **Technical Terms** and **Worry**. To check that Word has got it right, you can view the file properties and check how many words each document has.

- In the Open dialog box toolbar, click the **Properties** button.

- Use ⬇ to move down the list of documents, checking the number of words in each.

- When you have finished, click the **List** button.

- Click the **New Search** button.

Using a saved search

When you are looking for a file, it may often be appropriate to use a search you saved previously. There are two ways to access a saved search. First, open the Open dialog box. Then do one of the following:

- ✎ Click the **Commands and Settings** button, point to **Saved Searches** and click the name of the search. The search will start immediately.

- ✎ Open the search and then start it. Click the **Advanced** button, click the **Open Search** button, choose the search from the list and click **Open**. Then click the **Find Now** button.

This time, try starting the **More than 250 words** search using the **Commands and Settings** button. You can *open* a search later.

- Click the **Commands and Settings** button.

- Point to **Saved Searches**.

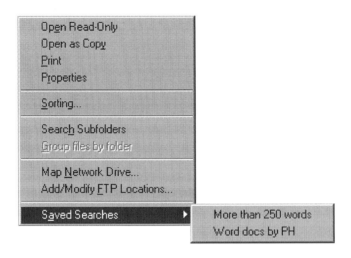

- Click **More than 250 words**.

Word carries out the search again and presents you with the list of files that match the search criteria.

Opening a search

If you want to edit a search, you have to *open* it. You need to display it in the Advanced Find dialog box. To do this:

- ↳ In the Advanced Find dialog box, click the **Open Search** button

- ↳ In the list of saved searches, choose the search you require

- ↳ Click **Open**

You can try this now.

- In the Open dialog box, click **Advanced**.

- In the Advanced Find dialog box, click the **Open Search** button.

The Open Search dialog box is opened. Here you can choose a particular search and then either open, rename or delete it. This time you can open the search **Word docs by PH**. Then you can edit it.

- Choose **Word docs by PH.**

- Click **Open,** or press **Enter.**

The search is opened and displayed in the Advanced Find dialog box.

Editing a search

You can add another criterion to the search. This time you will use the **Or** function. You want to search for files written by Peter Harrison *or* files that are over 300 words long.

- Check that **Author includes** *Peter Harrison* is currently selected.

- In the Define more criteria group of options, click **Or** so that it is chosen.

- Open the Property list box and choose **Number of words.**

- Open the Condition list box and choose **more than.**

- In the Value box, type:

  300

- Click **Find Now.**

Because you didn't click **Add to List** after you had specified the criterion, Word displays a message box. This asks if you would like to add this criterion to the search before leaving the Advanced Find dialog box. You should click **Yes**.

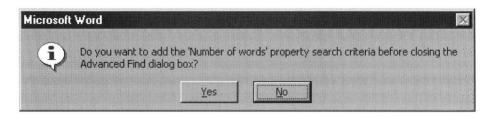

- Click **Yes**.

Word carries out the search for you and finds at least eight files that match the search criteria.

Deleting searches

All that remains now is to delete the two searches you have saved. This is done in the Open Search dialog box.

- Click **Advanced**.

- Click **Open Search**.

- In the list of searches, choose **More than 250 words**.

- Click **Delete**, then click **Yes** to confirm the deletion.

- Delete the search **Word docs by PH** in the same way.

- If necessary, click **Cancel**, or press **Esc**, to close the Open Search dialog box.

- Close the Advanced Find and Open dialog boxes.

On your own

Now you might like to experiment by doing a few searches for yourself. Perhaps you could search on your own name, or look for exercise files you have saved, using the wildcard options. When you have finished, remember to delete any searches you have saved, but no longer wish to keep.

Ending the session

You have now completed the tutorial in this chapter. You can either move on to the next chapter or exit Word.

●   `If you are not continuing directly with the next chapter and want to stop now, open the` **`File`** `menu and choose` **`Exit`** `to exit Word.`

Summary ~ Searching for Files

If you have a large number of documents, you may not always remember where you have stored them, or even what a particular file is called. Word provides a number of ways to search for a file or group of files. All searching takes place in the Open dialog box.

Drives and folders

    ✎   To change drives, open the <u>Look in</u> list box and click the icon for the drive you require

    ✎   Double-click a folder to open it

     ✎   Click the **Up One Level** button to move up a level

Simple file searches

Click the **New Search** button to reset the search criteria to their default values. Then choose from four simple search criteria. These are:

- **Filename** - type the name you are searching for in the File name box, or use an asterisk * in place of part of the name, then click **Find Now**.

- **File type** - open the Files of type list box and choose the file type you are looking for. If the required file type is not shown, type the DOS extension for that particular file type in the File name box. Click **Find Now**.

- **Text or property** - type the text or property you are looking for in the Text or property box, and then click **Find Now**.

- **Last modified** - open the Last modified list box and choose one of the alternatives: **today**, **this week**, **last month**, etc., and then click **Find Now**.

 There is also a **Search the Web** button, which, when clicked, will open the Search page of your Internet Browser if you have one.

Advanced file searches

To apply more selective search criteria, click the **Advanced** button in the Open dialog box. Use the **New Search** button to reset the defaults, and the **Delete** button to delete specific search criteria, highlighted in the Find files that match these criteria box.

To set new criteria:

- Decide whether you want the criterion to be **And** or **Or** with respect to any other criteria currently highlighted

- Open the Property list box and choose what you want to search on, e.g., Filename, Author, Number of words

- Choose the appropriate Condition

- If necessary, type a Value

      ↳   Click **Add to List**

Use the <u>Look in</u> list box to change the drive or folder to be searched, and then decide whether or not to **Search subfolders**. When you are ready to start the search, click **Find Now**.

Saving a search

To save a search, click the **Save Search** button in the Advanced Find dialog box. Name the search and click **OK**.

Starting a saved search

To start a saved search:

      ↳   Click the **Commands and Settings** button in the Open dialog box

      ↳   Point to **Saved Searches** and choose the search you require

Opening, editing and deleting a search

To open a saved search:

      ↳   Click the **Open Search** button in the Advanced Find dialog box, then choose the search from the list provided and click **Open**

To edit the search:

      ↳   Select any criterion you wish to remove, and click **Delete**, then add any additional criteria using the options in <u>Define more criteria</u>

To delete a search:

      ↳   Select it in the Open Search dialog box, and click **Delete**, then click **Yes** to confirm deletion

Notes

Use this page to make notes of your own.

Page #   Notes

_____   _____

_____   _____

_____   _____

_____   _____

_____   _____

_____   _____

_____   _____

_____   _____

_____   _____

_____   _____

_____   _____

_____   _____

_____   _____

_____   _____

Chapter 11 ~ Document Security

Occasionally, you may have a document that you want to keep to yourself, or at least try to discourage other users from changing. This chapter looks at the various options available to you.

In this chapter you will learn about:

- Different levels of security
- Read-only recommended files
- Password to modify
- Password to open
- Automatic save
- Automatic back up copies

Remember:

- If you use passwords you should have a system for recording them
- If you forget a password, you may lose access to the document completely
- Passwords are case sensitive, i.e., **duck** is not the same as **DUCK** or **Duck**

To get started

● If necessary, start your Word program.

Levels of security

If you are working with documents that are private, or sensitive, you may want to stop or restrict other users from accessing the documents. You may also have documents that you want others to see, but not be able to change. The levels of security are explained below:

    ✎   **Read-only recommended**. This means that you can see the file but not make changes. If a user opens a Read-only recommended file, Word shows a message saying it is recommended that it should be opened as read-only unless changes need to be saved.

    ✎   **Password to modify**. If a Password to modify has been set, anyone opening the document will be asked for the password. If they enter the correct password they will be able to change and save the document. If they are unable to enter the correct password, they will be able to look at, and print, the document, but not save any changes.

    ✎   **Password to open**. If a Password to open has been set, only users who know the password will be able to gain access to the document.

Read-only recommended

You should be starting with a new document.

●   If necessary, click the **New** button.

You can now enter some text.

●   Type:

```
Document Security

This document is only used to investigate
the read-only feature.
```

To make a file Read-only recommended, you must save the file. (If you are protecting a document that has already been saved before, you must use the **Save As** menu option.) Save the current file on your exercise diskette with the filename **Secure1**.

- Make sure your exercise diskette is in drive A.

- Open the **File** menu and choose **Save As.**

- In the File name box, type:

  a:Secure1

You will now set the **Read-only recommended** option.

- Click the **Options** button.

The Save dialog box is displayed showing the Save options.

Security options

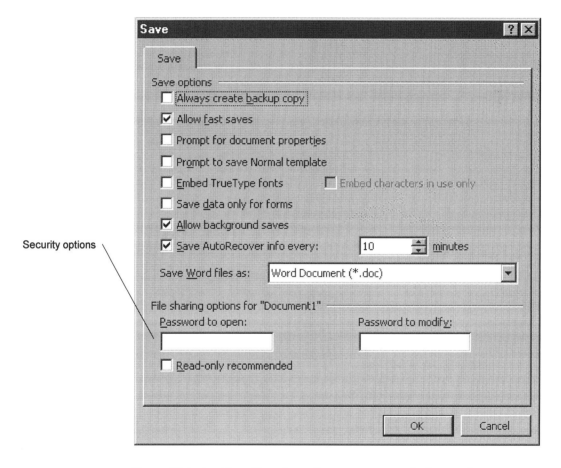

- Click the **Read-only recommended** option so that it is ticked.

- Click **OK.**

The Save As dialog box is visible again.

- Click **Save,** or press **Enter,** to save the document.

To try the feature out, close the file and then open it again.

● Open the **File** menu and choose **Close**.

● Open the **File** menu and choose **Secure1** – it should be number **1** in the list of recently opened files.

A message box is displayed.

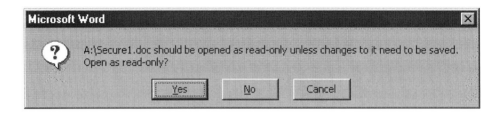

Remember, this is only a *recommendation* so you can choose:

    ✎   **Yes** to open the file as read-only, or **No** to open the file and be able to save changes

● Click **Yes** to open the file as read-only.

Now you will make some changes to the document, and then try saving them.

● Move to the end of the document (**Ctrl+End**).

● Press **Enter** twice to create some new lines, then type:

I'm changing it!

You can make changes, and print them out, but you can't save the file.

 ● Open the **File** menu and choose **Save,** or click the **Save** button, or just press **Ctrl+S**.

No! You're not allowed to save the changes.

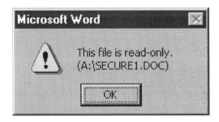

- Click **OK**.

The Save As dialog box is displayed giving you a chance to save the changed document with a new filename. Don't do this now.

- Click **Cancel,** or press **Esc,** to close the Save As dialog box.

Finally, close the document again.

- Open the **File** menu and choose **Close** – don't save the changes.

Changing a Read-only recommended file

Even though a file may be Read-only recommended, it is only a recommendation, so you can still open it and make and save changes. You will now open it and temporarily remove the Read-only recommendation.

- Open the **File** menu and choose **Secure1** – it should be number **1** in the list of recently opened files.

A message box is displayed.

- Click **No,** to open the file not as read-only.

The document is opened, but not as read-only and you should be able to change it and save the changes.

- Move to the end of the document (**Ctrl+End**).

- Press **Enter** twice to create some new lines, and type:

  This time I am changing it!

- Open the **File** menu and choose **Save,** or click the **Save** button, or just press **Ctrl+S.**

Yes! This time the changes are saved. You can now close the document.

- Open the **File** menu and choose **Close.**

Just to check that the file is still read-only, try opening it again.

- Open the **File** menu and choose **Secure1** from the list of files.

The message box is displayed again.

- Click **Yes** to open the document as read-only.

You will notice that the changes that you made when you opened the document not as read-only, have been saved. You can finish off by closing the document.

- Open the **File** menu and choose **Close**.

Password to modify

A Password to modify is set in a similar way to the Read-only recommendation. Again, you need to open a new document and add a short text.

- Click the **New** button.

- Type:

   This document is used to investigate the Password to modify feature.

Save the document, with the filename **Secure2**, on your exercise diskette.

- Make sure your exercise diskette is in drive A.

- Open the **File** menu and choose **Save As**.

- In the File name box, type:

   a:Secure2

Now you will set the **Password to modify** option.

- Click the **Options** button.

The Save dialog box is displayed again.

- Click the Password to modify box so that you get a flashing insertion point.

- Type:

  plum

Note that the password is shown as ****; this is in case someone is looking over your shoulder!

- Click **OK**.

The Confirm Password dialog box is displayed.

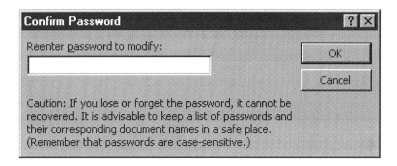

You need to type the password in again to make sure that you have entered it correctly.

- Type:

  plum

Again the password is shown as ****.

- Click **OK**, or press **Enter**.

If the password was the same both times you typed it in, it will be accepted. If there was a difference, neither password will be accepted and you will have to start again. When the password is correct you are returned to the Save As dialog box.

- Click **Save**, or press **Enter**, to save the document.

To try the feature out, close the file and then open it again.

- Open the **File** menu and choose **Close**.

- Open the **File** menu and choose **Secure2** - it should be number **1** in the list of recently opened files.

The Password dialog box is displayed.

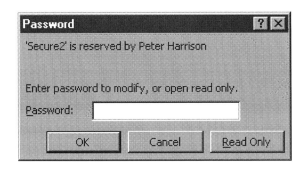

Password

'Secure2' is reserved by Peter Harrison

Enter password to modify, or open read only.

Password:

OK   Cancel   Read Only

↳ If you know the password, you can type it in the <u>Password</u> box. You will then be able to change the document and save it.

↳ If you don't know the password, you can click **Read Only**. You will then be able to change and print the document, but not save the changes.

This time, you will enter the password.

● In the <u>Password</u> box, type:

  plum

● Click **OK**, or press **Enter**.

Assuming you didn't make a mistake with the password, either when you saved the document, or now when you are opening it, the document will be opened for you. If you type the wrong password, you will be told it is incorrect and can try again.

You will now finish off by closing the document.

● Open the **File** menu and choose **Close**.

Printing a password to modify document

Assume you would like to modify a particular document and print it. However, the document is protected by a password that you do not know. You can opt to open the document as read-only, make the changes you require and print it. You would have to save the document to a new filename to save the changes you made. Try it out now:

● Open the **File** menu and choose **Secure2** from the list of documents.

● Click the **Read Only** button.

- Move to the end of the text and insert two blank lines.

- Type:

  Can I print this document even though it is read-only?

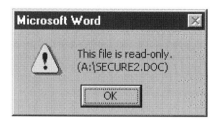

- Click the **Print** button.

The document will be printed with your changes. Now try saving the document.

- Open the **File** menu and choose **Save**, or click the **Save** button, or press **Ctrl+S**.

You will see a message box reminding you that the file is read-only.

Microsoft Word

⚠ This file is read-only.
(A:\SECURE2.DOC)

OK

- Click **OK**.

The Save As dialog box is displayed. You can save the document with a new name, **Secure2 - Changed**.

- In the File name box, type:

  a:Secure2 - Changed

- Click **Save**, or press **Enter**.

The document is saved with a new filename that can be seen in the Title bar. Finally, you can close the document.

- Open the **File** menu and choose **Close**.

Password to open

The final level of security is Password to open. Setting a Password to open means you have to have the password even to look at the file, let alone change it. The process is similar to the Password to modify feature.

- Click the **New** button.

- Type:

  This document will be protected by a password.

Save the document, with the filename **Secure3**, on your exercise diskette.

- Make sure your exercise diskette is in drive A.

- Open the **File** menu and choose **Save As**.

- In the File name box, type:

  a:Secure3

Next you will set the **Password to open** option.

- Click the **Options** button.

The Save dialog box is displayed again.

- Click the Password to open box so that you get a flashing insertion point.

- Type:

  cherry

- Click **OK**.

The Confirm Password dialog box is displayed, and you need to type the password in again to make sure you got it right.

- Type:

  cherry

- Click **OK**, or press **Enter**.

You are returned to the Save As dialog box.

- Click **Save**, or press **Enter**, to save the document.

To try the feature out, close the file and then open it again.

- Open the **File** menu and choose **Close**.

- Open the **File** menu and choose **Secure3**.

The Password dialog box is displayed.

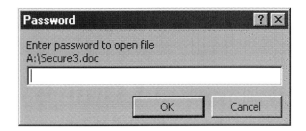

This time there is no **Read Only** button. You either have the password and can access the file, or you don't get to open the file.

- In the Enter password to open file box, type:

  cherry

- Click **OK**, or press **Enter**.

The document is opened.

Save AutoRecover & Back up copy options

There are two options available that are also connected with the security of your documents, not against unwanted readers, but against what can happen if your computer goes down. These options are set via the **Tools**, **Options** menu option, or by choosing **Options** in the Save As dialog box.

- Open the **Tools** menu and choose **Options**.

The Options dialog box is displayed.

- If necessary, click the **Save** tab to show those options.

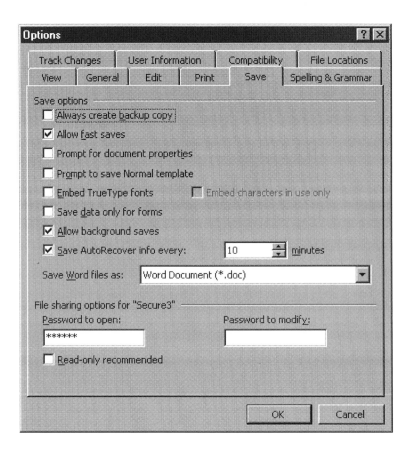

Save AutoRecover

Using the Save AutoRecover feature, you can instruct Word to make a copy of the current document at regular intervals, for example, every 10 minutes. This means that in the event of the computer going down, your document would have been saved ten minutes ago, at the most. To set this option:

    ✎   Make sure the **Save AutoRecover info every** option is ticked

    ✎   Enter the time period in the <u>minutes</u> box

If your computer goes down when you are working on a particular document, Word will have saved a copy of your document. When you restart the computer, Word will offer you the recovered version of the document; that is, the latest version from its automatic saves.

Back up

If you have the back up option enabled, when you save a document, Word keeps the previous version of the document that was saved, by creating a new file. This file has the name 'Backup of filename'. So, if the original file was called **Happy**, the back up copy is renamed to **Backup of Happy**. In the event of a computer failure and your **Happy** file being lost or damaged, you could open the **Backup of Happy** file. Similarly, if you wanted to abandon the most recent changes you saved, you could revert to the previous version of your document, **Backup of Happy**.

To set this option in the Options dialog box:

> ✎ In the **Save** set of options, make sure the **Always create backup copy** option is ticked

For now, just close the Options dialog box without making any changes.

● Click **Cancel,** or press **Esc.**

To open the back up copy of a particular document:

> ✎ Open the **File** menu and choose **Open**

> ✎ In the <u>Files of Type</u> list box, choose **All Files**

> ✎ Double-click the icon or filename of the back up copy

Ending the session

You have now completed the tutorial in this chapter. There are three additional exercises that you may wish to do before moving on to the next chapter or exiting Word. First, you should close the current document.

● Open the **File** menu and choose **Close** – choose **No** to avoid saving the changes.

● If you are not continuing directly with the extra exercises or the next chapter and want to stop now, open the **File** menu and choose **Exit** to exit Word.

Exercise 11a

First, practise opening a document as read-only. Then make changes to the document and save it with a new name.

- Open the **Document Security 1** document from your exercise diskette as read-only.

- Move to the bottom of the document and create two blank lines, then type:

  I have changed this document so I am going to save it with a new name.

- Click the **Save** button.

- When presented with the message box, click **OK**.

- Save the document with the new filename **a:Document Security 1 - Changed**.

- When you are ready, close the document.

Exercise 11b

Now, you will open the **Document Security 2** document from your exercise diskette. It has the password APPLE.

- Open the **Document Security 2** document from your exercise diskette.

- When prompted, type the password:

  APPLE

If you could not open the document, try again, remembering that the password is in upper case letters.

- When you are ready, close the document without making any changes.

Exercise 11c

Finally, try creating a document with a protection password yourself.

- Open a new document.

- Type:

  I am going to save this document with a protection password. I hope I will remember the password when I come to open the document again.

- Open the **File** menu and choose **Save As**.

- In the File name box, type:

  a:Document Security 3

- Click the **Options** button.

- In the Password to open box, type:

  bananas

- Enter the password again when prompted.

- Click **Save,** or press **Enter,** to save the document.

- When you are ready, close the document.

Now try opening the document using the password you have set.

- Open the **File** menu and choose **Document Security 3** from the list of files – when prompted, enter the password:

  bananas

- When you are ready, close the document.

Summary ~ Document Security

Word provides three levels of protection for your documents against other users: Read-only recommended, Password to modify and Password to open. To protect your work from total loss should your computer go down, you can use automatic save and automatic back ups.

Read-only recommended files

When a file is Read-only recommended, a user can choose whether to view it as read-only and not be able to make changes, or open it as not read-only and make changes.

To save a document as read-only recommended:

- ✎ Open the **File** menu and choose **Save As**

- ✎ Click the **Options** button

- ✎ Click the **Read-only recommended** option so that it is ticked

To open a read-only recommended document, click **Yes** to view without making changes; click **No** to open the document and make changes.

Password to modify

If the **Password to modify** option is set, anyone who enters the correct password can change and save the document. If they are unable to enter the correct password, they can view the document as read-only.

To set the **Password to modify** option:

- ✎ Open the **File** menu and choose **Save As**

- ✎ Click the **Options** button

- ✎ Type the required password in the <u>Password to modify</u> box

- ✎ Confirm the password in the Confirm Password dialog box

To open the document, type the correct password when prompted, or click the **Read Only** button.

Password to open

If the **Password to open** option is set, the document can only be opened by someone who knows the correct password. To set the **Password to open** option:

- ✎ Open the **File** menu and choose **Save As**

- ✎ Click the **Options** button

- ✎ Type the required password in the <u>Password to open</u> box

- ✎ Confirm the password in the Confirm Password dialog box

To open the document, type the correct password when prompted.

Save AutoRecover

With the Save AutoRecover feature enabled, Word will make a copy of the current document every few minutes. This is set in the **Save** set of options in the Options dialog box (**Tools**, **Options**). You can choose how frequently you want Word to make the AutoRecover saves.

If your computer goes down while you are working on a particular document, Word will have a recent copy of your document saved. When you restart the computer, Word will offer you the recovered version of the document; that is, the latest version from its AutoRecover saves.

Automatic back up copies

With **Always create backup copy** enabled, Word will automatically save the previous version of a document to a new name, 'Backup of filename'. This is set in the **Save** set of options in the Options dialog box (**Tools**, **Options**). Should you lose your current version of a particular document, you can open the back up version.

Notes

Use this page to make notes of your own.

Page #   Notes

_____   _____

_____   _____

_____   _____

_____   _____

_____   _____

_____   _____

_____   _____

_____   _____

_____   _____

_____   _____

_____   _____

_____   _____

_____   _____

_____   _____

Chapter 12 ~ Creating a Letter Template

Templates are very useful for creating standard documents that you produce frequently. In this chapter, you will create a letter template.

In this chapter you will cover the following points:

- ✎ Setting page margins

- ✎ Adding and formatting a header and footer

- ✎ Adding the date

- ✎ Writing the letter and formatting the text

- ✎ Saving the template as a Document Template

- ✎ Using the template

It is assumed that:

- ✎ You have the general skills up to an intermediate level - none of the items covered are new, and instructions are kept short

To get started

- If necessary, start your Word program.

- If the Office Assistant is displayed at any time throughout this chapter, you should read what it has to say and then close it – click the **Close** button in the Office Assistant window.

You should be starting with a new blank document.

- If necessary, click the **New** button.

Page setup

The starting point for a letter template should be the page size and its margins. If you are using letterhead paper, you will want to set the margins so that the text area does not run over anything already printed on the letterhead paper.

In this example, the template will include a company name as a header at the top of the page, and address, telephone and fax numbers as a footer at the bottom. Suitable margins would be 2.54 cm (1 inch) left, right and bottom and 6.35 cm (2.5 inches) at the top, with header and footer margins of 1.9 cm (0.75 inches).

● Open the **File** menu and choose **Page Setup**.

The Page Setup dialog box is displayed. You need to display the **Margins** tab.

● If necessary, click the **Margins** tab to show those options.

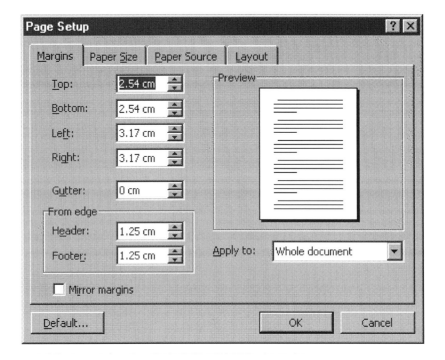

● Change the Top margin to **6.35** cm, or **2.5** inches.

● If necessary, change the Bottom, Left and Right margins to **2.54** cm or **1** inch.

- Change the Header and Footer margins to **1.9** cm or **0.75** inches.

You should now have a large margin at the top of the page.

- Click the **Paper Size** tab to show those options.

- Make sure the correct paper size is chosen.

- Make sure the **Portrait** option is chosen.

- Click **OK**.

Adding a header and footer

You will now add a company name as a header and format it.

- Open the **View** menu and choose **Header and Footer**.

- In the Header box, type:

  LearnFast Limited

- Format the text to be **36pt, bold** and **italic**.

The header should now resemble the next picture.

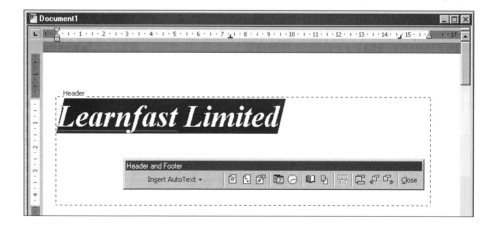

Next, you will add the footer and format it.

- In the Header and Footer toolbar, click the **Switch Between Header and Footer** button.

- In the Footer box, type:

  Unit 4, Wedgewood Place, MINEHEAD, TA45 3YY.

- Press **Enter**.

- Type:

  Tel:01234-567890 Fax:01234-567891

Now format the footer:

- Format both lines of text as **9pt** and centre them.

Finally, you will add a line above the footer.

- Click the downward-pointing arrow in the **Borders** button to display the box of border buttons.

- In the box of border buttons, click the **Top Border** button.

A line now appears above the footer, and the header and footer are now complete.

- In the Header and Footer toolbar, click **Close**.

If you are in the Normal view, you will not see the header and footer you have created.

- If necessary, open the **View** menu and choose **Page Layout**, or click the **Page Layout View** button.

You can see the header now: it is shown in a grey text to indicate it is the header and not part of the main body of text. If you scroll the document downwards you will see the footer too. If you have the background spell checker running, you will also see a red wavy line under any words that Word does not recognise. You can ignore these, unless you have mis-spelt them!

Save the document

Before going further, it is a good idea to save your work. Later, you will save the document as a Document Template in the Templates folder for Word. However, for now, save the document on your exercise diskette.

- Save the document on your exercise diskette with the name **a:My Letter Template**.

Typing the details of the letter

Now it is time to add the letter details including Your ref, Our ref and a date field. When you create your own template, you may want a different arrangement altogether.

- Type, with a space after it:

  Your ref:

- Press **Enter** twice.

- Type, with a space after it:

  Our ref:

- Press **Enter** twice.

Now add a date field, letting Word put in today's date for you.

- Type, with a space after it:

  Date:

- Open the **Insert** menu and choose **Date and Time**.

The Date and Time dialog box is displayed.

- Choose the date style you require.

If you want the date to be correct every time you print the document, make sure the **Update automatically** option is ticked.

- If you wish, click **Update automatically** so that it is ticked.

- Click **OK**.

- Press **Enter** three times.

Adding address lines and salutation

The next step is to add the address lines. This is information that will change from letter to letter.

- Start by typing a line for the Addressee:

  Addressee

- Press **Enter**.

- Type the following address, pressing **Enter** after each line:

  Job title/dept
  Company name
  Address line 1
  Address line 2
  Town
  Postcode

- Press **Enter** a further three times.

- Type, with a space after it:

  Dear

- Press **Enter** twice.

Typing the letter

All that is left now is to type the body of the letter.

- Type the letter as follows (let Word take care of the line breaks, but press **Enter** to conclude paragraphs and create empty lines as indicated):

  Thank you for your telephone enquiry today regarding the availability and price of our forthcoming products. The expected release dates and prices are shown below and we will write to you again, as each product becomes available.

  [Enter x 2]

```
Microsoft PowerPoint 97 Beginners,
available February 1997, price £25.00
                              [Enter]

Microsoft Access 97 Beginners, available
March 1997, price £25.00
                              [Enter]

Microsoft Access 97 Intermediate, available
April 1997, price £25.00
                              [Enter]

Microsoft Outlook 97, available June 1997,
price £26.50
                          [Enter x 2]

Normal discounts, etc., will apply.
[Enter x 2]

If you would like further information on
these or any of our range of products,
please call me.
```

- Press **Enter** twice and type:

  Yours sincerely,

- Press **Enter** four times.

- Type your name, for example:

  Samantha Goulding

- Click the **Save** button, or press **Ctrl+S**.

Formatting the text

Now, make a few small changes to the text:

- If necessary, format the text as **12pt**.

- Justify the main paragraphs of the letter.

- Format the line starting <u>Normal discounts</u> as **bold**.

- Format the name you typed at the end of the letter as **underlined**.

To make the list of products available stand out more clearly, give them bullets:

- Select the four product lines - the first one starts <u>Microsoft PowerPoint</u>.

- Click the **Bullets** button.

Bullets are inserted on all four lines. You have now finished creating the letter template. However, it is advisable to run a spelling and grammar check before you save the document again.

- Click the **Spelling and Grammar** button.

- Follow the spelling and grammar check - you will have to make your own decisions about what it suggests.

- When you are ready, click the **Save** button, or press **Ctrl+S** to save the document.

- Use **Print Preview** to view the document.

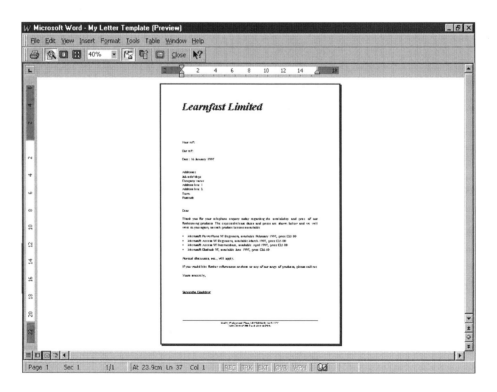

- When you are ready, click **Close** to return to the document.

Saving the template in Word

When you create a standard letter in Word, it is useful to save it as a Document Template in the **Templates** folder, on the hard drive of your computer. Then, the next time you want to send a standard letter, you can open the New dialog box and choose the template for that letter.

To save a document as a Document Template:

    ✎   Open the Save As dialog box (**File**, **Save As**)

    ✎   In the <u>Save as type</u> list box, choose **Document Template**

    ✎   Enter the name you require for the template in the <u>File name</u> box

    ✎   Click **Save**

As usual, the best way to learn is by example. Save the **My Letter Template** document to the Templates folder with the name **My Letter**. (Do not worry about saving the template to the hard drive of your computer; you will be instructed to delete it at the end of this tutorial.)

●   Open the **File** menu and choose **Save As**.

●   Open the <u>Save as type</u> list box and choose **Document Template**.

Because you have chosen the Document Template file type, the <u>Save in</u> box shows the default folder for templates, **Templates**.

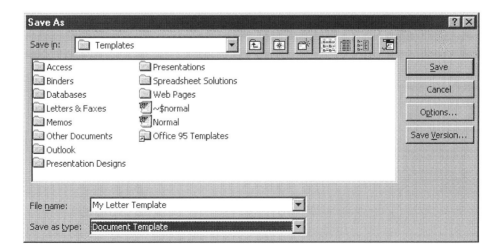

- In the File name box, change the name to:

  My Letter

- Click **Save,** or press **Enter.**

Your letter is saved as a template. You can try it out but first, close the current document.

- Open the **File** menu and choose **Close.**

Using the template

It is now time to use the template. This involves opening the template, adding references, entering the name and address and adding the salutation. Then you can save the letter and print it.

- Open the **File** menu and choose **New.**

The New dialog box is displayed. It displays the templates that are available to you: the **Blank Document** template for Word, your **My Letter** template and any other general templates stored in the Templates folder in your computer.

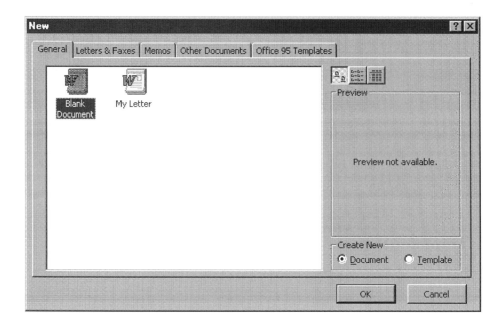

> *You may have additional templates displayed in your New dialog box.*

- Double-click the **My Letter** icon.

My Letter

The standard letter is opened. You can now modify it for your current addressee. Assume that there is no Your ref: detail to be added, but you want to add some Our ref: details.

- Position the insertion point at the end of the Our ref: line.

- Type your initials and some other detail, e.g.:

SG/PMP/9411

The date is filled in automatically by Word. Now, select each address line in turn and type the new details.

- Type the new details for the addressee, e.g.:

Addressee	**Ms K Wyndale**
Job title/dept	**The IT Training Manager**
Company name	**Sherlock Training plc**
Address line 1	**Baker Street House**
Address line 2	**High Street**
Town	**YORK**
Postcode	**YO9 2RR**

> *Another time, if any address line is not applicable, you may wish to delete the line altogether, and then add an extra blank line before or after the address.*

Now add the salutation:

- Position the insertion point at the end of the Dear line.

- Type a salutation, with a comma after it, e.g.:

Ms Wyndale,

The letter is now complete. You should save it on your exercise diskette before you print it.

- Save the letter on your exercise diskette with the filename **a:Letter to Ms Wyndale.**

- Make sure your printer is on and ready to print.

- Click the **Print** button.

Your letter is printed and ready to sign. A copy of the letter is shown on the next page.

●   `When you are ready, close the document.`

Another way of doing it

Another way of working with a template would be to set up the document template as the main document in a Mail Merge. Names and addresses would be stored as a data source document. You could then replace the address lines with merge fields, and use Mail Merge to print personalised letters.

LearnFast Limited

Your ref:

Our ref: SG/PMP/9411

Date: 14 January 1998

Ms K Wyndale
The IT Training Manager
Sherlock Training plc
Baker Street House
High Street
YORK
YO9 2RR

Dear Ms Wyndale,

Thank you for your telephone enquiry today regarding the availability and price of our forthcoming products. The expected release dates and prices are shown below and we will write to you again as each product becomes available.

- Microsoft PowerPoint 97 Beginners, available February 1997, price £25.00
- Microsoft Access 97 Beginners, available March 1997, price £25.00
- Microsoft Access 97 Intermediate, available April 1997, price £25.00
- Microsoft Outlook 97, available June 1997, price £26.50

Normal discounts, etc., will apply.

If you would like further information on these on any of our range of products, please call me.

Yours sincerely,

Samantha Goulding

Finishing off

The template you have just created is stored on your hard disk. As it is unlikely that you will want to write any more letters with this particular template, you should delete it. This is easily done in the New dialog box. There are four simple steps to follow:

    ✎   Open the **File** menu and choose **New**

    ✎   Right-click the icon for the template you want to delete

    ✎   Choose **Delete** in the shortcut menu

    ✎   Click **Cancel**, or press **Esc**, to close the New dialog box

You can delete the **My Letter** template now.

My Letter

- Open the **File** menu and choose **New**.

- Right-click the **My Letter** icon and choose **Delete**.

A message box is displayed asking you to confirm the deletion.

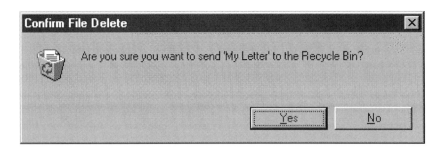

- Read the message carefully to check you are going to delete the correct template.

- When you are sure, click **Yes**.

- Click **Cancel**, or press **Esc**, to close the New dialog box.

Ending the session

You have now completed the tutorial in this chapter. There is an additional exercise that you may wish to do before moving on to the next chapter or exiting Word.

● If you are not continuing directly with the extra exercise or the next chapter and want to stop now, open the **File** menu and choose **Exit** to exit Word.

Exercise 12a

In this exercise you will open a standard fax template, modify it for your own use, and then save it to the Templates folder with a new name. You will then open it. Finally, if you no longer need this particular template, you can delete it from your hard drive.

● Open the **File** menu and choose **New**.

● Click the **Letters & Faxes** tab to show those templates.

Because you are going to create a new template, not a new document, you need to click the Template option.

● In the Create New group of options, click **Template** so that it is chosen.

Professional
Fax

● Double-click the **Professional Fax** icon.

You are presented with a fax template, which you can now modify to suit your company.

● Select the text Company Name Here and type your own company name, for example:

Ladderless Treefellers

● Click the [Click here and type return address and phone and fax numbers} text on the top line of the document, and type your company address and telephone and fax numbers. For example:

**42 West Side, BIRMINGHAM, B11 4RD
Tel: 01234-234234 Fax: 01234-234235**

● Select the text and format it as **10pt bold**.

- Within the form, insert any details that will be the same every time you send a fax, for example, your name.

If you have a company logo, you might like to add it in the bottom right-hand corner of the page.

- Move to the bottom of the page.

- Use **Insert, Picture, From File** to insert a picture - there is a picture on your exercise diskette you can use if you like (**Leaves.wmf**).

- If necessary, move and resize the picture.

When you are satisfied with your fax template, you can save it with a new name, **My Fax**.

- Click the **Save** button, or press **Ctrl+S**.

The Save As dialog box is displayed.

- Open the Save as type list box and choose **Document Template**.

- In the File name box, type:

  My Fax

- Click **Save**, or press **Enter**.

The document is saved as a new template. Before you try it out, close the current document:

- Open the **File** menu and choose **Close**.

Now, open a new document with the **My Fax** template.

- Open the **File** menu and choose **New**, then click the **General** tab to show those options.

My Fax

- Double-click the **My Fax** icon.

You can now edit the new document and print the fax if you wish. Then close the document.

- Close the current document without saving the changes.

If you do not want to keep the template you have created, you should delete it now.

- Open the **File** menu and choose **New**.

- Right-click the **My Fax** icon and choose **Delete,** and then click **Yes** to confirm the deletion.

- Click **Cancel,** or press **Esc,** to close the New dialog box.

Summary ~ Creating a Letter Template

Templates are very useful for creating standard documents that you produce frequently. For your everyday routines, you may find it helpful to create a number of templates for standard letters, faxes, tables and forms.

Creating a letter template

To create a letter template for a standard letter:

- Set up the margins for the paper you intend to use

- Include your company name, address, telephone and fax numbers as a header/footer

- Use **Insert**, **Date and Time** to insert a date field

- Type the text that you require and format it accordingly

- Run the spell checker before you save the template to ensure there are no errors

Saving a standard letter as a Document Template

If you save the letter template as a Document Template in the **Templates** folder, it will be available as a template in the New dialog box. To save a document as a template:

- Open the **File** menu and choose **Save As**

- In the Save as type list box, choose **Document Template**

↳   Type the name you require in the <u>File name</u> box

↳   Click **Save**, or press **Enter**

Using a Document Template

To use a template stored in the Templates folder:

↳   Open the **File** menu and choose **New**

↳   If necessary, click the **General** tab

↳   Double-click the icon for the template you require

↳   Edit the new document that is opened, as appropriate

Deleting a Document Template

To delete a Document Template you no longer require:

↳   Open the **File** menu and choose **New**

↳   Right-click the icon for the template and choose **Delete**

Notes

Use this page to make notes of your own.

Page #   Notes

_____   _____

_____   _____

_____   _____

_____   _____

_____   _____

_____   _____

_____   _____

_____   _____

_____   _____

_____   _____

_____   _____

_____   _____

_____   _____

_____   _____

Notes

Use this page to make notes of your own.

Page #   Notes

——————— ——————————————————————————

——————— ——————————————————————————

——————— ——————————————————————————

——————— ——————————————————————————

——————— ——————————————————————————

——————— ——————————————————————————

——————— ——————————————————————————

——————— ——————————————————————————

——————— ——————————————————————————

——————— ——————————————————————————

——————— ——————————————————————————

——————— ——————————————————————————

——————— ——————————————————————————

——————— ——————————————————————————

——————— ——————————————————————————

Chapter 13 ~ An Introduction to Macros

Word offers two ways of creating macros: the macro recorder and the Visual Basic Editor. In this chapter, you will learn how to create a couple of macros using the macro recorder. You will also perform a couple of simple edits in the Visual Basic Editor.

In this chapter you will cover the following points:

- ✎ What macros are
- ✎ Creating a macro to insert a phrase
- ✎ Replaying a macro
- ✎ Editing a macro
- ✎ Creating a macro to open a document
- ✎ Deleting a macro

To get started

- If necessary, start your Word program.

- If the Office Assistant is displayed at any time throughout this chapter, you should read what it has to say and then close it – click the **Close** button in the Office Assistant window.

You should be starting with a new blank document.

- If necessary, click the **New** button.

What is a macro?

Sometimes you will find yourself typing the same text, or following the same sequence of actions many times over. Rather than repeating the same actions every time, you can *record* them once in a *macro* - this stores the actions and makes them available to you to use whenever you want. Each time you need to repeat the sequence of actions, you simply *replay* the macro and the whole process is completed for you automatically.

You can record as many macros as you like. If you have many repetitive tasks, you can build up a whole library of macros - this should result in an increase in productivity.

Creating a macro

In this first example, you will create a simple macro to finish off a letter. You need to type the text in once, which you can do in the current document.

- Open the **Tools** menu and choose **Macro,** then choose **Record New Macro.**

The Record Macro dialog box is displayed.

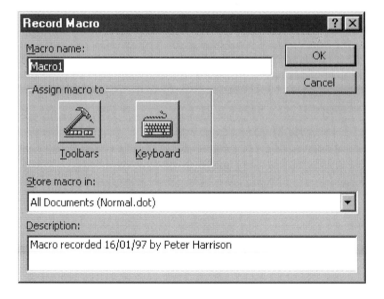

Before continuing, you need to give your macro a name and decide how to assign it, i.e., how to be able to choose it when you want to use it. In this case you will call the macro **SignOff** and assign it to the keyboard with the key combination **Alt+1**.

●   In the <u>Macro name</u> box, type:

     SignOff

> ✎   *The <u>Macro name</u> can be up to 80 characters long, but cannot contain spaces or symbols.*

●   Select the current entry in the <u>Description</u> box, and type:

     Sign off a letter

●   Click the **Keyboard** button.

Yet another dialog box, Customize Keyboard, is displayed.

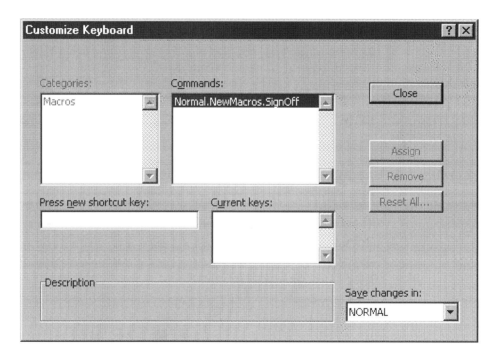

All you need to do is to choose a key combination for your macro. You will use **Alt+1**. If this is already in use you will have to choose another combination. Try using **Ctrl+B** first to see the effect of using a combination that is already assigned.

●   Press **Ctrl+B**.

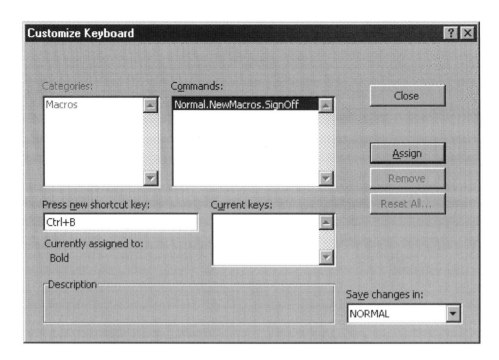

The combination is currently assigned to applying bold text so you can't use it.

- Press the **Backspace** key to delete the **Ctrl+B** combination.

- Press **Alt+1** – if this combination is already assigned, delete it and choose another.

- Click the **Assign** button.

- Click **Close**.

The dialog box is closed now. You are returned to your document ready to record the macro. The mouse pointer has changed and there is a small Stop Recording toolbar in the document. This is used to pause or end the recording.

- Move the Stop Recording toolbar down towards the bottom of the screen – this will not be part of the macro.

- Type:

  Yours sincerely

- Press **Enter** 4 times.

- Press **Ctrl+U** to turn on underlining.

- Type:

  Amanda Mason

- Press **Ctrl+U** again to turn off the underlining.

- Press **Enter**.

- Type:

  for and on behalf of Fuzzy Widgets Ltd

- Click the **Stop Recording** button in the Stop Recording toolbar.

Replaying a macro

Don't believe it until you see it! Try out the macro. Clear the current document first and then open a new one.

- Open the **File** menu and choose **Close** – don't save the changes.

- Click the **New** button.

- Type:

  I've just finished my letter.

- Press **Enter** twice.

- Press **Alt+1** (or whatever combination you used for the macro).

Can you believe it now!

- Open the **File** menu and choose **Close** – don't save the changes.

Editing a macro

You can edit a macro. Some things are easy, like changing the text a little. Other aspects need more understanding of the special Visual Basic language that Word uses - this is not covered in this course. In this case, assume that you want to add a comma after <u>Yours sincerely</u> and a full stop after <u>Ltd</u> in the last line.

● Open the **Tools** menu and choose **Macro,** then choose **Macros.**

The Macros dialog box is displayed.

● In the list of macros, choose **SignOff.**

● Click the **Edit** button.

Word now opens the Microsoft Visual Basic Editor, which has a window with the macro details in. Don't worry too much about the Visual Basic language surrounding the words you wish to edit - you will just be concentrating on changing the text within the speech marks ("").

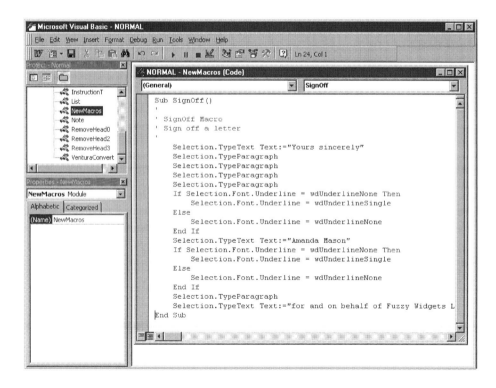

● Move the insertion point immediately after the word <u>sincerely</u> (but before the speech marks).

- Type a comma:

  ,

- Move the insertion point immediately after the word <u>Ltd</u> (but before the speech marks) – you may have to use the horizontal scroll bar in the macro window.

- Type a full stop:

  .

Now save this macro file and then close it:

- Click the **Save** button, or press **Ctrl+S**.

- Open the **File** menu and choose **Close and Return to Microsoft Word**.

Now, try the macro again. First, you need to open a new blank document.

- Click the **New** button.

- Type:

  I've just finished another letter.

- Press **Enter** twice.

- Press **Alt+1** (or whatever combination you used for the macro).

The new text with comma and full stop is inserted.

- Open the **File** menu and choose **Close** – don't save the changes.

Creating a macro to open a document

Macros aren't limited to inserting phrases. In this second example, you will create a macro that opens the **Home Security** document from your exercise diskette.

- Open the **Tools** menu and choose **Macro**, then choose **Record New Macro**, or just double-click the **REC** button in the Status bar.

The Record Macro dialog box is now displayed.

- In the <u>Macro name</u> box, type:

  OpenHomeSecurity

- Replace the current entry in the <u>Description</u> box, with:

  Open the Home Security document

- Click the **Keyboard** button.

The Customize Keyboard dialog box is displayed.

- Press **Alt+2** - if this combination is already assigned, delete it and choose another.

- Click the **Assign** button.

- Click **Close**.

You can now start recording the macro.

- Make sure your exercise diskette is in drive A.

- Click the **Open** button, or press **Ctrl+O**.

The Open dialog box is displayed.

- In the <u>File name</u> box, type:

  a:Home Security

- Click **Open**, or press **Enter**.

The document should be opened and you can stop recording.

- Click the **Stop Recording** button in the Stop Recording toolbar.

Try it out

Now it's time to try out the macro. Start by closing the document. You can then use the macro to open it again.

- Open the **File** menu and choose **Close**.

- Press **Alt+2** (or whatever combination you used for the macro).

After a short wait, the document is opened.

Deleting a macro

To finish off the chapter, you will delete the two macros you created.

- Open the **Tools** menu and choose **Macro,** then choose **Macros.**

The Macros dialog box is displayed.

- In the list of macros, choose **OpenHomeSecurity.**

- Click the **Delete** button.

Word asks you to confirm the deletion.

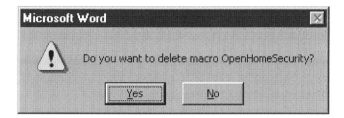

- Choose **Yes.**

- In the list of macros, choose **SignOff.**

- Click the **Delete** button.

Word asks you to confirm the deletion.

- Choose **Yes.**

- Click **Close** to close the Macros dialog box.

Ending the session

Congratulations! You have now completed the tutorial in this final chapter. It was a very brief introduction to macros, a world of automation that could save you a lot of time and effort! There are two additional exercises that you may wish to do before exiting Word. First, you should close the current document.

- Open the **File** menu and choose **Close** – choose **No** to avoid saving the changes.

- If you are not continuing directly with the extra exercises and want to stop now, open the **File** menu and choose **Exit** to exit Word.

Exercise 13a

Suppose you have taken over from someone who used a rather dated layout and font for their documents. It is your job to update all these documents. A quick way to do this would be to write a macro.

- Open the **Home Security** document from your exercise diskette.

- If necessary, click the **Show/Hide ¶** button to show the paragraph markers.

As you will see, this document is in Courier New 12pt, with the spacing between paragraphs provided by an extra carriage return. You will record a macro that changes the document to Times New Roman 12pt with a 6pt space between paragraphs, and format the heading as 16pt, bold, underlined and centred. You will then use this macro to change the **Costa del Fortune** document. This happens to be formatted in the same way.

- Open the **Tools** menu and choose **Macro,** then choose **Record Macro,** or just double-click the **REC** button in the Status bar.

- Call your macro **TidyUp,** and give it the description:

  Removes blank lines and reformats text

- Click the **Keyboard** button.

- Assign the shortcut key **Alt+3** (or another combination if this is already assigned).

- Click **Assign** and then click **Close.**

You are now ready to record the macro. Remember, every keystroke and mouse click you make, from now on, is recorded.

- Press **Ctrl+A** to select the whole document.

- Change the font to **Times New Roman.**

- Press the ↑ key.

The insertion point should now be at the start of the first line. You can now remove the extra line breaks. This is done by using Replace All.

- Open the **Edit** menu and choose **Replace**, or just press **Ctrl+H**.

- Delete any entry that may already be in the Find what box.

- If necessary, expand the Find and Replace dialog box by clicking the **More** button.

- Click the **Special** button and choose **Paragraph Mark**.

- Click the **Special** button and choose **Paragraph Mark** again.

- Click the Replace with box and delete any entry that may already be there.

- Click the **Special** button and choose **Paragraph Mark**.

You are now ready to replace each occurrence of two paragraph marks with one, thereby removing the blank line between paragraphs.

- Click **Replace All**.

- When prompted, click **OK**.

- Then click **Close** to return to the document.

Now change the paragraph formatting of the body of the text:

- Press the ↓ key to move to the start of the first paragraph.

- Hold down the **Shift** key and press **Ctrl+End**.

The remainder of the document is selected.

- Open the **Format** menu and choose **Paragraph**.

- In the Paragraph dialog box, set the following:

Indentation Special	**First line**	By
1cm		
Spacing Before	**6pt**	
Alignment	**Justified**	

- Click **OK**.

The paragraphs should now have a first line indent of 1cm and have a half line space between them. Finally, you should reformat the heading.

- Move the insertion point to the start of the first line of the document (**Ctrl+Home**).

- Press **Shift+End** to select the line.

- Format the heading as **16pt, bold, underlined** and **centred**.

- Click the **Stop Recording** button in the Stop Recording toolbar.

- Click the **Show/Hide ¶** button to hide the non-printing characters.

You can now close this document without saving the changes, and try out your TidyUp macro on **Costa del Fortune**.

- Close the document without saving the changes.

- Open the **Costa del Fortune** document.

- Make sure the insertion point is at the start of the document.

- Take a deep breath and press **Alt+3** (or the key combination you chose for the TidyUp macro).

Lo and behold the document is reformatted before your very eyes! Amazing! If you would like to see it again, just close the document without saving the changes and run the macro a second time. Or try it out on the **Home Security** document.

When you have finished, you should delete the macro.

- Open the **Tools** menu and choose **Macro,** then choose **Macros.**

- In the list of macros, choose **TidyUp.**

- Click the **Delete** button – choose **Yes** to confirm the deletion.

- Click **Close** to close the Macros dialog box.

- Close the document without saving the changes.

Exercise 13b

As a final exercise in this course, award yourself a Certificate of Achievement.

- Open the **Certificate** document from your exercise diskette.

- Select the line Type your name in here and type your name.

- Make any other changes you would like to see.

- Print the document, then close it without saving the changes.

Summary ~ An Introduction to Macros

Macros provide a way of storing sequences of instructions you do frequently in Word. You record the series of keystrokes and mouse clicks required to accomplish the task. You can then run the macro when you next want to undertake that particular task.

Recording a macro

To record a macro:

- Open the **Tools** menu and choose **Macro**, then choose **Record New Macro**

- Name the macro and give it a description

- Assign a shortcut key combination to the macro

- Click **Close** to return to the document

- Carry out the keystrokes and mouse clicks required

꙳ Click the **Stop Recording** button in the Stop Recording toolbar

Replaying a macro

꙳ If necessary, position the insertion point at the correct place in the document

꙳ Press the shortcut key combination

Editing a macro

꙳ Open the **Tools** menu and choose **Macro**, then choose **Macros**

꙳ Choose the macro you wish to change and click **Edit**

The Visual Basic Editor is opened.

꙳ Make the necessary changes to the instructions

꙳ Save the changes (**File, Save**)

꙳ Close the Visual Basic editor and the macro file (**File, Close and Return to Microsoft Word**)

Deleting a macro

꙳ Open the **Tools** menu and choose **Macro**, then choose **Macros**

꙳ Choose the macro you wish to delete and click **Delete**

꙳ Click **Close** to close the Macro dialog box

Notes

Use this page to make notes of your own.

Page #   **Notes**

———————   —————————————————————————

———————   —————————————————————————

———————   —————————————————————————

———————   —————————————————————————

———————   —————————————————————————

———————   —————————————————————————

———————   —————————————————————————

———————   —————————————————————————

———————   —————————————————————————

———————   —————————————————————————

———————   —————————————————————————

———————   —————————————————————————

———————   —————————————————————————

———————   —————————————————————————

———————   —————————————————————————

Notes

Use this page to make notes of your own.

Page #   Notes

_____   _____

_____   _____

_____   _____

_____   _____

_____   _____

_____   _____

_____   _____

_____   _____

_____   _____

_____   _____

_____   _____

_____   _____

_____   _____

Notes

Use this page to make notes of your own.

Page #   Notes

_____   _____

_____   _____

_____   _____

_____   _____

_____   _____

_____   _____

_____   _____

_____   _____

_____   _____

_____   _____

_____   _____

_____   _____

_____   _____

_____   _____

Notes

Use this page to make notes of your own.

Page #   Notes

_____ _____

_____ _____

_____ _____

_____ _____

_____ _____

_____ _____

_____ _____

_____ _____

_____ _____

_____ _____

_____ _____

_____ _____

_____ _____

_____ _____

_____ _____

The PC User Certificate Series

At last you can learn to use a particular software package at home, at work or through a training provider, and then take a short assessment test to gain a certificate that is recognised nationally. Certification normally costs between £20 and £25. For more information contact:

Phone, normal office hours and ansafone: 01635 529193
Fax: 01635 46512
E-mail: kol@newbury-college.ac.uk
Web site for complete listing of certificate titles, new developments and send-back enquiry form: http://www.newbury-college.ac.uk/kol/pcuser1.htm

The certification process is outlined below.

1. Study the course
Learn your chosen software program using one of *Peter Harrison's PC Training Courseware* packages. This can be done at your own pace, on any PC - at home, at work, or through a training provider.

2. Register for the assessment
Fill in the registration provided and send or fax it together with the *appropriate* fee to the designated assessment centre. You will receive the assessment pack within a few days. To save time, you can register before you have finished studying the course.

3. Do the assessment test
You can do the assessment test on any PC - at home, at work, or through a training provider. You will need to answer some questions on paper and save some practical tasks on disk. The assessment will normally take between 1 and 3 hours to complete.

4. Return the assessment pack
When you have completed the assessment tasks, you should return the required documents and disks to the assessment centre.

5. Get your certificate
You should be notified of your result within 14 days. A Statement of Competence and an official certificate will follow. If you fail, you can retake all or part of the assessment when you are ready.

Q&A about the PC User Certificate series

Who developed the PC User Certificate series?
Newbury College has developed the PC User Certificate series.

Who validates the certificate?
The *Southern Regional Council for Education and Training*, which is recognised as a validating body by the Department for Education and Employment, validates the PC User Certificate series.

What does the qualification lead to?
A PC User Certificate provides you with evidence of competence, which you can use to gain NVQs, thereby increasing your employment opportunities.

Where does the assessment take place and what does it include?
The assessment test can be taken on any computer - at home, at work, or at a training centre. It is based on real tasks and includes a multiple-choice section and practical exercises to be saved on disk.

The PC Crash Course Series

For details about the **PC User Certificate Series**, check the previous page.
The following books are available in the PC Crash Course Series:

ISBN	Title	Subtitle	Release Date	Price
187300530X	Computers & the Internet	Beginners Course	15/12/98	£22.95
1873005318	Microsoft Windows 98	Beginners Course	15/11/98	£22.95
1873005326	Microsoft Word 97	Beginners Course	15/11/98	£22.95
1873005334	Microsoft Word 97	Intermediate Course	15/11/98	£22.95
1873005342	Microsoft Word 97	Advanced Course	15/11/98	£22.95
1873005350	Microsoft Excel 97	Beginners Course	15/11/98	£22.95
1873005369	Microsoft Excel 97	Intermediate Course	15/11/98	£22.95
1873005377	Microsoft Excel 97	Advanced Course	15/11/98	£22.95
1873005385	Microsoft PowerPoint 97	Beginners Course	15/11/98	£22.95
1873005393	Microsoft PowerPoint 97	Intermediate Course	15/11/98	£22.95
1873005415	Microsoft Access 97	Beginners Course for Users	15/11/98	£22.95
1873005423	Microsoft Access 97	Beginners Course for Developers	15/11/98	£22.95
1873005431	Microsoft Publisher 98	Beginners Course	15/11/98	£22.95
187300544X	Microsoft Works v4.5	Beginners Course	15/11/98	£22.95
1873005458	Microsoft Works v4.5	Word Processing Intermediate Course	15/11/98	£22.95
1873005466	Microsoft Works v4.5	Spreadsheets Intermediate Course	15/11/98	£22.95
1873005474	Microsoft Works v4.5	Databases Intermediate Course	15/11/98	£22.95
1873005482	Corel WordPerfect v8	Beginners Course	15/11/98	£22.95
1873005490	Corel WordPerfect v8	Intermediate Course	15/11/98	£22.95
1873005504	Corel WordPerfect v8	Advanced Course	15/11/98	£22.95
1873005512	Sage Instant Payroll v4	Beginners Course	15/11/98	£22.95
1873005520	Sage Instant Accounting 98	Beginners Course	15/11/98	£22.95
1873005539	Sage Line 50 v5	Financial Controller Beginners Course	15/02/99	£22.95
1873005547	Sage Line 50 v5	Financial Controller Intermediate Course	15/02/99	£22.95
1873005555	Sage Line 50 v5	Financial Controller Advanced Course	15/02/99	£22.95
1873005563	Sage Line 50 v5	Accountant Plus Beginners Course	15/02/99	£22.95
1873005571	Sage Line 50 v5	Accountant Plus Intermediate Course	15/02/99	£22.95
187300558X	Sage Line 50 v5	Accountant Beginners Course	15/02/99	£22.95
1873005598	Lotus Word Pro v9	Millennium Edition Beginners Course	15/03/99	£22.95
1873005601	Lotus Word Pro v9	Millennium Edition Intermediate Course	15/03/99	£22.95
187300561X	Lotus Word Pro v9	Millennium Edition Advanced Course	15/03/99	£22.95
1873005628	Lotus 1-2-3 v9	Millennium Edition Beginners Course	15/11/98	£22.95
1873005636	Lotus 1-2-3 v9	Millennium Edition Intermediate Course	15/11/98	£22.95
1873005644	Lotus 1-2-3 v9	Millennium Edition Advanced Course	15/03/99	£22.95
1873005652	Lotus Freelance Graphics v9	Millennium Edition Beginners Course	15/03/99	£22.95
1873005660	Lotus Freelance Graphics v9	Millennium Edition Intermediate Course	15/03/99	£22.95
1873005679	Lotus Approach v9	Millennium Edition Beginners Course	15/03/99	£22.95
1873005687	Lotus Approach v9	Millennium Edition Intermediate Course	15/03/99	£22.95
1873005695	Microsoft Word 2000	Beginners Course	30/04/99	£22.95
1873005709	Microsoft Word 2000	Intermediate Course	30/04/99	£22.95
1873005717	Microsoft Word 2000	Advanced Course	30/04/99	£22.95
1873005725	Microsoft Excel 2000	Beginners Course	30/04/99	£22.95
1873005733	Microsoft Excel 2000	Intermediate Course	30/04/99	£22.95
1873005741	Microsoft Excel 2000	Advanced Course	30/04/99	£22.95
187300575X	Microsoft PowerPoint 2000	Beginners Course	30/04/99	£22.95
1873005768	Microsoft PowerPoint 2000	Intermediate Course	30/04/99	£22.95
1873005776	Microsoft Access 2000	Beginners Course for Users	30/04/99	£22.95
1873005784	Microsoft Access 2000	Beginners Course for Developers	30/04/99	£22.95

The exercise diskette

An exercise diskette accompanies this course. It should be stuck to the back cover
opposite. If it is missing or damaged, your bookshop will be able to get a
replacement for you.

> ✍ *The exercise diskette contains practice files used in the book. There are no*
> *programs to install and it has no commercial value.*